WE MUST STOP MEETING LIKE THIS

We Must Stop Meeting Like This

MEIC PEARSE and CHRIS MATTHEWS

KINGSWAY PUBLICATIONS

EASTBOURNE

ISBN 0 85476 796 7

Published by:
KINGSWAY PUBLICATIONS
Lottbridge Drove, Eastbourne, E Sussex, BN23 6NT.
E-mail: books@kingsway.co.uk

Designed and produced for the publishers by
Bookprint Creative Services, P.O. Box 827, BN21 3YJ, England.
Printed in Great Britain.

Contents

Preface

Many of the ideas in this book were floated during a teaching-session-with-feedback in Swansea which Meic led and Chris chaired. The meeting was so enthusiastic about some of the material that we had a brainwave . . . and this book is it! How much of a brainwave it really was only time – and, perhaps, book-sales – will tell. We are well aware of the sharp intakes of breath that parts of the book are likely to provoke. We have queried no evangelical articles of faith (far from it – we affirm them), but we have done something that many will find even harder to forgive: we have called into question some of the central assumptions of what it means to be 'church'.

For offence caused, we ask forgiveness. We believe, however, that many others will be relieved, even delighted, that they are not alone in their growing alienation from the evangelical culture of meetings, nor alone in their suspicions that that culture is looking increasingly untenable. We hope that, amidst our criticisms, we have also laid sufficient emphasis upon the really positive and hopeful developments in the present situation!

Inevitably, we have incurred some debts. Thanks are due to Karen Chalk for hitting upon a great title and for acting as a sounding-board for ideas. In the latter capacity, rather a lot of London Bible College students should also be mentioned, but the group around Rachie, Holger, Claire and friends were certainly not backward in coming forward with their opinions – for which many thanks. We are grateful for permission from *The New Christian Herald* to re-use material in Chapter 7 which was previously published as an article in that paper.

Most of all, thanks are due to our wives, Ann and Barbara, for making space, for carrying even more than the usual burdens in other spheres so that this could be finished, and for generally keeping us in order. Whatever would we do without you? Hopefully, we will never find out!

1

Churches in a Choosy Society

> It was the best of times, it was the worst of times . . . it
> was the epoch of belief, it was the epoch of incredulity, it was
> the season of Light, it was the season of Darkness, it was the
> spring of hope, it was the winter of despair . . . in short,
> the period was so far like the present. . . (Charles Dickens,
> *A Tale of Two Cities*)

Looking back on the French Revolution, Charles Dickens
wryly observed that then, as in his own day, people had
been torn between hope and despair. In the process, he
was inviting his readers to recognise the universality of
this mental disposition. It's hard not to recognise ourselves in the mirror he sets before us. At the turn of the
millennium, in the vortex of worldwide change –
technological, economic, moral and, perhaps most of
all, cultural – there is today also much to be thankful for,
as well as much cause for alarm and consternation.

Evangelical Christians have generally tended to be pre-
disposed to alarm in whatever situation they have found
themselves, and to draw unfavourable comparisons with

the past, which was always better, always more godly than the iniquitous present. To be sure, evangelicals are not the only ones to have reasoned this way, though in recent centuries they have sometimes come close to cornering the market in declamatory pessimism, at least in their pronouncements about the condition of 'the world'. Concerning their own condition, analyses have been more various, ranging from similar morbid nostalgia to outright triumphalism.

This is not a book about the state of the world, but about the state of the evangelical church within it. Is this a good time for evangelicalism, or a bad one? Is hand-wringing over the present and idealising of the past in order – or should we be sounding a note of triumph? To be sure, there are positive signs enough. In Britain, at least, there has been healthy growth for over a generation now. In America, evangelicals have invaded the political scene in ways that have incited controversy, not least among themselves, but which are certainly high profile. The church in Africa, Latin America and even parts of Asia such as South Korea and China, is seeing explosive growth. The shackles of communism have collapsed in Eastern Europe, opening at least a window of opportunity there. The culture around us in the West may be more secular than ever, but the falling away of nominal adherents has left the tolerably orthodox in prime possession of the 'Christian' tag. When politicians start laying claim to it – as a number have started to do again recently, even in Britain – they are unavoidably owning up to belief in a transcendent God, rather than just to a fatuous social respectability. To start evangelising one's neighbours twenty-five years ago was to risk being mistaken for a Jehovah's Witness; nowadays we may be no more welcome, but folks have a clearer idea of who we are. The waves of charismatic renewal have sharpened the commitment and deepened the experience of many Christians, and have created a general atmosphere of expectation and faith for better things to come. The God who heals and speaks in prophecy will surely not leave his people to languish in insignificance and decline!

The renewed confidence is evidenced in dozens of different ways, both big and small. 'March for Jesus' is a clear attempt to go public and impress with numbers, and points away from the 'little flock' mentality of the mid-century. The use of modern music in worship is now often without reserve, a situation many miles removed from the dance-and-cinema-shunning ideas of unworldliness that characterised an earlier generation of Christians. The burgeoning numbers of Christian publications, the large conferences, the new church buildings, the Christian CDs, tapes and radio stations are all signs of growth and its accompanying optimism. The sharp decline (in Britain, the virtual collapse) of dispensational teaching with its any-minute rapture theory is in large part a rejection of the pessimism about evangelical prospects in the here-and-now that made such doctrines so attractive during the period of evangelicalism's eclipse. The theological faculties of the universities have been, if not quite reclaimed, at least reoccupied; evangelical scholarship is no longer an oxymoron, and the best evangelical colleges are no longer ghettos whose sole purpose is to protect their students from critical questioning. In short, everything about the evangelical renaissance exudes a renewed confidence, a 'can do' mentality that stands in sharp contrast to the self-protective foetal position it has displaced.

'It was the best of times, it was the worst of times.' If the progress has been impressive, there is nevertheless a looming crisis for evangelicalism which is already making itself felt. In the first place, evangelism in Western countries is becoming harder and harder for a number of related reasons. The logic of the cult of 'privacy' makes all religion an essentially private affair, an unwelcome intruder into the public domain except, perhaps, as an assurance of a politician's personal integrity. (Tony Blair's churchgoing is a public signal that he's a decent chap, and not a radical leftie; the idea that it may inform his policies on abortion or privileging heterosexual marriage is as much anathema as it would have been had he been a declared atheist.) Religion may be true for you, but not for me.

Similarly, the privatisation of morality makes Christian ethical claims appear intolerant, unintelligible or simply ridiculous. The one moral idea which does demand widespread support (even if there is little agreement about its actual content), that of human rights, makes it equally hard for people to see themselves as sinners. Only if I recognise that I have obligations am I able to see myself as having failed to fulfil them, and so as morally deficient. If I have only rights, I am much more likely to see myself as sinned against – the victim mentality. The first prerequisite of evangelism – the ability to see oneself as a sinner in need of a Saviour – is absent, and Christianity is once again rendered unintelligible or else ridiculous.

Western society is now well into the second, or perhaps even the third, generation in which privatisation, human rights and the absence of moral absolutes are considered self-evident truths. Evangelism, unsurprisingly, is becoming increasingly hard work. Growth in those Western countries where evangelicalism has been historically marginal, such as most of continental Western Europe, is slender indeed.

The second problem is internal to the church, but is symptomatic of the wider society in which it exists. That is the extremely low, and diminishing, level of commitment to institutions, or even to personal relationships. Very few Christians consider themselves committed to a particular denomination. The fact that a Baptist church contains members who were christened as babies, rather than baptised as believers, is no longer a sure sign that it is on the slippery slope to liberalism; it is simply an accommodation of the evangelical Anglicans who have moved into the area, or who preferred their worship style to that of St Justin's up the road. A mirror image of this situation exists in many evangelical Anglican churches without anyone calling in the bishop to discipline those who have been 'rebaptised'. Denominational diehards are a dying breed; far more people perceive themselves as belonging to the evangelical community as a whole, or to some broad strand within it, such as 'charismatic', 'Reformed', 'house church' or whatever.

This flexibility is not in itself a problem; it might be

seen as a very good thing. However, it comes about as a result of constant shifting from one congregation to another. Much of this is the result of the geographical mobility – people moving jobs from one part of the country to another – that is such a marked feature of the middle classes, in which evangelicalism has been historically stronger. But not all of the church-switching comes from job-and-house-switching. A huge amount is the result of disaffection, arguments or the endless hunt for greener grass. This has been a growing problem for at least a generation, but increasingly we are witnessing people giving up on 'church' altogether without, they would claim, giving up on Christ.

The third problem is the massive cultural shift that is taking place under our feet and all around us. It is the dreaded 'p'-word: postmodernity. It is not an ideology, but an instinctive mistrust of all ideologies, including ours. It is not itself a culture, but rather the insistence that all cultures can be mixed and matched. It is not an ethic, but rather a tendency to assume that no ethical claims have any wider significance than that of the group norm. Postmodernity is a set of attitudes that affects millions of people who could never articulate these thoughts or even spell 'postmodernity'. It is the air we breathe, the vague collection of presuppositions that is increasingly making up what unreflective people will call 'common sense'.

And if it is making evangelism difficult, it is making acceptance of our church culture downright impossible. It is now common sense that every institution can justify its existence only on pragmatic grounds and the continuing approval of those who wish to belong to it. No institution – not even a church – is sacred in the sense of being a 'given' from the past, requiring our obedience now and our faithful bequeathing of it to posterity. If Christians don't like the arrangements in their church – whether its form of government, its leaders, its building or (most of all) its meetings – they will say so. Their criticisms may be sound or mistaken, well-motivated or self-seeking, but fewer and fewer of them will accept defences of the *status quo* based solely upon the authority of the institution or its leaders.

Facing the culture gap

It's a funny thing, but one of the biggest hindrances to evangelism is the church. We've recognised it for a long time. Our evangelistic approaches say 'Don't look at the church, look at Jesus.' And the reason we talk about 'low-cringe' events and 'cringe-free' evangelistic meetings is because most of our services, to be honest, would make anybody cringe. Of course, we Christians put up with it, even though it drives us to distraction most of the time and we come home to our Sunday lunches complaining about this, that and the other thing.

Even if we're 'spiritual' (however that is defined by our particular brand of evangelicalism), we know, in our heart of hearts, that taking a non-Christian friend along to our services would be unlikely to convert them. If we're *that* sort of evangelical, we know full well that listening to one of the Reverend Elwyn Rhys-Lewis's hour-long discourses on a phrase in 1 Chronicles would probably not convince an unchurched person that they ought to become a Christian. And if we're the *other* sort of evangelical, the prospect of subjecting a work colleague or neighbour to all that hysterical laughter and people hyperventilating on the floor would, we know, leave us with more explanation on our hands than we would have faced before.

We're not the first to face the problem. It's been creeping up on us for well over a century. The urban poor felt completely out of place in many of the middle-class chapels of the Victorian nonconformists. The Salvation Army was founded as a sort of buffer to convert the poor without subjecting them to an alien culture – or at least, not subjecting them straight away. But the cultural gap proved unbridgeable, and the short-term expedient of a mission hall turned into a long-term denomination. A lot of individual tin tabernacles turned into smaller versions of the same thing. And that was back in 'the good old days' when Christian ideas were common currency.

In more recent years, when Christianity has been viewed with an increasing mixture of mistrust and incomprehension, youth clubs have functioned as (fairly) ideal ways of reaching teenagers who would never come to our services. Young people have been converted and, all too frequently, fallen away again as the awful realisation dawned on them that, not only would they have to forsake sin, but they would have to go 'in there and join that lot', the latter challenge mostly proving as great as the former.

How do we get out of this situation? Over the past twenty years or so we have spawned a raft of new churches whose rallying cry has been 'culturally relevant worship', and a whole host of older congregations have made the same move, often after splits or bitter internal struggles. There have been a lot of gains from this, though frequently at the expense of alienating older people. The changes in the church often caused friction and heart-searching but, for a while at least, they seemed to do the trick. However, even here payday has rolled around – as it has a habit of doing – and several problems are now apparent.

By and large, we have simply created a different, groovier sort of cultural Christian ghetto, which non-Christians find only marginally easier to relate to than the Moody-and-Sankey-hymn-sandwich that was there before. Some who have been in the new, or 'renewed', churches for ten or twenty years are getting bored with it. Youngsters, too, are as likely as not to smirk at the un-groovy grooviness of rock churches dominated by people who are now in their forties and fifties. Teenagers who've been brought up in them don't see them as 'cool' at all; I mean, whatever your parents do is bound to be so much old hat, isn't it?

It's also hard not to conclude that at least some of the warnings by the old diehards about the absence of teaching have been proved correct: Bible knowledge in the trendier churches has gone the way of spelling and times tables in the trendier schools, with expression winning out over content every time. Not that traditionalists can take any comfort of an 'I-told-you-so' kind from the growing discomfiture of 'happy-clappy' churches; society is moving on, not back towards a receptivity to expository sermons and hymn sandwiches. The challenges facing us are new ones. Going back to being two generations out of date, rather than just one, is simply not an option.

The problem of keeping those we have

So where do we go from here? Recent years have seen the rise of 'performance praise' and 'rave worship' styles, particularly among the young, with the usual mixture of pretty impressive new material and fatuous rubbish being used as vehicles for praise and devotion. (But remember, Charles Wesley had his 'off' days too!) In marketing terms, these are nothing more than 'extension strategies': an old product is revitalised, but only temporarily, by the addition of new gizmos, a differently coloured wrapper or a choice of new flavours. In any case, the hi-tech raves are too elaborate and expensive to be produced on a sustained basis by most local churches. The necessary degree of sophistication, resources and talent is simply not available at a local level. In the same way, lots of ordinary Sunday school teachers have put themselves through unnecessary condemnation at their failure to be another Ishmael. Worship concerts are, by their nature, feasible only at the level of occasional productions in at least relatively large venues. To be sure, all the churches of a big town might come together to produce something of the sort. Even so, would any responsible Christian want to suggest that large-scale praise-ups should be the staple spiritual fare of young Christians and the primary expression of what it means to 'be church'?

What's the answer to this problem? Meetings that are so worldly they're just like an evening down the pub? A very few churches have even tried this approach. It's not without its appeal, but somehow we're unlikely to see it catching on universally.

In the meantime, even many long-time Christians are starting to drop out of church meetings that just seem so far removed from their out-of-meetings experience, or that they find irritating for some other reason. Many young Christians make the break when they go away to college. The temptations there to backslide are obvious, of course. One of the authors teaches at a Bible college where the backsliding rate is (as one might hope!) a lot lower, yet even here the opt-out from church attendance continues. Many find it very difficult to find a church whose overall culture they feel they can accept, fit into and submit to. And almost always their dissatisfaction centres upon meetings.

One group of recent university graduates cut the Gordian knot on this issue. The range of local churches off campus had been limited and none had seemed attractive, so as students they had started to meet on their own for worship and fellowship. When graduation day wheeled around and college came to an end, they decided collectively that they were not going to join up with any church. They all wanted to continue their walk as Christians but, as far as church was concerned, they went their separate ways and simply dropped out.

If they felt lonely, they shouldn't have. There are so many like them. Some friends of one of the authors recently made a decision to leave their church. Bob and Sandra are a middle-aged married couple who had been faithful members for years. There had been no crisis, either in their personal lives or in the church, and their own faith was as solid as ever. Yet they had no idea which church they would go to instead; this was a case of *flight from* what they perceived to be a bad situation, rather than *flight to* a good one. And the reason? They had become fed up with the worship style in the church meetings. Either it had changed over the years, or they had, or both. They 'didn't get anything out of the services'. It would be easy to take a judgemental view of Bob and Sandra, and we certainly don't agree with what they are doing. One of us tried, and failed, to talk them out of it. The irritation with the way things were had just become too much.

Of course, if the number of dissatisfied people in a congregation make common cause (behind a particular programme or a leader), there is likely to be a split. This has always happened, but again the rate at which it is happening is increasing. It's no accident that it is in America, where consumer choice has been the greatest for the longest, that the number of denominations is higher than anywhere else on earth. But in Britain also, churches, especially the more radical ones, are constantly splitting. Once again, the issues are usually connected with the character of meetings and who leads them. Such crises have become so frequent that there is a market for books and advice on how to head off such splits.[1]

---

[1] See eg, D. Bridge, *How to Spot a Church Split Before It Happens (and do something about it)* (Monarch, 1989); J. & N. Rye, *The Survivor's Guide to Church Life* (IVP, 1992); H.F. Halverstadt, *Managing Church Conflict* (Westminster/John Knox Press, 1991); E. Towns, *Putting an End to Worship Wars* (Broadman & Holman, Nashville, 1997).

Anglicans, of course, are above problems of this sort. Unlike the radical churches, *they* do not split. They simply have an 8.00 a.m. service from the 1662 *Book of Common Prayer*, a middle-of-the-road family service at 10.30 a.m. and a Wimberised rave-up for the young folks on a Sunday night!

But with or without splits, the constant defection of the ones and twos is serious enough. One church known to us has about 200 members, having grown from around 30 in the mid-1970s. If that growth sounds impressive, the through-put has been even greater. Perhaps 500 people have been associated with – or counted as members of – the church during the intervening years. During the 1980s, the congregation was constantly gaining new members, but hardly grew at all. The reason? People were leaving out of the back door as fast as they were coming in the front.

A certain town on the outskirts of London is proverbial among pastors and church leaders for the constant circulation of Christians moving from one church to another, and then to another. It may be an extreme example, but what is happening there is happening everywhere, all the time. People are leaving your church and ours. Most of them (fortunately) are simply going somewhere else. Some, like the students we mentioned, weren't 'going' anywhere at all, but at least they were keeping the faith in their own isolated fashion (though it should be said that it's not much easier being a Christian on your own than it is to be a football player while never playing in a team). But a significant minority are checking out and dropping out completely. They are disillusioned by their experiences, hardened to the gospel, and bitter.

Why do people switch churches?

Whatever their destination, why do people move on? Any long-time Christian reading this book could trawl through their own memories of people who have left the church they belong to – or of churches that they themselves have left. Every story would be different. Blame, too, might be differently shared, mostly according to who was telling the story. Few churches would come well out of the stories told by those who have left them: 'The way that church operated was unbelievable!' And few leavers would come well out of the stories told by those who remained: 'Well, there was someone who *really* needed to sort themselves out with God!'

But maybe we should listen most to the leavers, *not* because they're more likely to be right, but because they're the ones whose stories count. In a free country, no one at all can make a person stay when they have decided to leave! The leavers may be wrong (though it's supremely unlikely that they *all* are), and in any case, they mostly want different, contradictory things. Placating some will simply alienate others. Indeed, this fact alone highlights the frustrating, almost impossible position in which most of our church leaders find themselves for much of the time. But the very phenomenon of so many switchers should tell us something. Why, in their own estimation at least, do they go?

The large majority of their stories, if you listen to

them, fall into three main categories. Many, like Bob and
Sandra, leave out of dissatisfaction with the style of the
meetings, particularly with the style of worship or the
quality of the preaching. Charismatics don't like traditional worship styles, non-charismatics (and even many
charismatics) are left cold by some of the manifestations
associated with the 'Toronto Blessing'. Traditionalists
don't like jazzed-up music, free-churchers can't stand
liturgy, young people detest the hymns, old folks can't
hear their own voices above the drum kit. . . You name it
– there are any number of reasons! Sermons are too long.
Or too short. They are not expository, and so are 'not
truly rooted in the Word'. Or they are tedious rhetorical
discourses, or shouting matches, or flippant, or delivered
by people who constantly repeat themselves, or who
don't know enough to be preachers at all. And of course
all of this is extremely irritating, going on as it does
Sunday after Sunday. What is worse, few of us live near
to enough churches to do any better than make a compromise on what suits us.

The second reason that people leave churches is over
issues of leadership. This may be as simple as a dislike of
the minister. But it may be the result of a dispute with the
leaders, of some deep-seated unease with their character
or the direction in which they are taking the church . . .
or frustration at their failure to take it anywhere at all.
On the other hand, it might reflect the leaders' disinclina-
tion to take the church where the person leaving had
wanted it to go, or their failure to give him or her enough
space to try a little leadership themselves. Indeed, the
losers in many of our fratricidal wars of church politics

often end up leaving, whether over real principle or simply because they can't handle the loss of face. This is as true of would-be elders as it is of ousted committee members of the flower-arranging rota. But the dissatisfaction with leaders almost always centres upon something that is done – or not done – by them in meetings, with their style of preaching, speaking or whatever.

The third reason that people tend to leave churches is the more general social one of 'not having my needs met'. This may be because there aren't enough like-minded others, or people of the same age-range and sex (or of the opposite sex!) as the person with itchy feet. Perhaps there are not enough children of similar age to those of the couple leaving. Or perhaps there are, but they are all abominably badly behaved and so the Sunday school is a nightmare. Perhaps the person feels socially marginalised. Perhaps there has been a breakdown of relationships. All reasons of this sort we can categorise under the general heading of 'social needs'. Even here, however, it tends to be the meetings that are the focus of dissatisfaction for the failure to 'meet needs'.

Now if all of this sounds quite unconscionably consumerist, this is because that is what we are. We have been brought up with the attitudes of consumers, and we don't change the thought patterns of a lifetime simply because we now happen to be selecting and staying with – or not staying with – a church. The authors are not in the business of preaching or prescribing how Christians ought to behave – at least not just yet. For the moment, we are simply describing how they *do* behave. It is vitally important to bear this point in mind, for our instinct as

Christians when faced with church conflict is to identify who is in the right and who is in the wrong, and then apply pressure to the latter to 'sort them out'. The problem with that, of course, is that we all have different perspectives, and are constantly falling out with one another over exactly who *is* 'in the right' or 'in the wrong'. Our instincts, in other words, tend to have the net effect of sucking us instantly into the vortex of the dispute and lending our weight to one side or the other. As a result, we end up just fanning the flames. Our best alternative strategy is to try to coax people to some sort of compromise, which often achieves little more than deferring the resolution of whatever issue was causing conflict.

That is why, in this book, we are adopting a different approach. In looking at the causes of conflict, we are addressing the issue of 'Why is this thus? What is the reason of this thusness?'[2] To be sure, we will be making recommendations. We will also, alas, be identifying some things that we consider to be 'wrong'. But we want to do this in a way that does not simply castigate certain categories of people for failing to 'get their act together', or leaders for failing to 'do it right', or church-switchers for being 'uncommitted' or 'rebellious'. Indeed, to listen to some analyses of church problems, one might be led to think that older Christians were to blame for being old, or young people for being young, or quiet types for failing to be 'free in worship' or extroverts for being 'irreverent'.

---

[2] Artemus Ward, 19th-century American humorist.

We dare to suggest that many of our problems are the result of much wider problems than many of us have been prepared to allow, and that they will not go away simply by raising our voices at one another.

The fact is that all of us have grown up in a society in which our range of choices is unprecedentedly large. Returning missionaries and visitors from the Third World have been known to burst into tears on entering a supermarket for the first time: it's not simply that they're overwhelmed by Western opulence, but that they are paralysed by the immensity of choice. So many different kinds of coffee! So many different brands of detergent! And what's true in supermarkets is true in the rest of our lives: what subjects we will study, what colleges we will go to, what careers we will enter, where we will go on holiday, what car we will buy. All of this choice partly reflects our high standard of living, and partly creates it. Because suppliers have to compete for our custom, they have to make their goods and services the best and cheapest they can be . . . or at least an optimal combination of those two qualities.

The trouble is, we transfer the same mindset to our relationships. We choose our friends and discard them when it suits us. This was never an option before the Industrial Revolution, when most people lived in small villages and never met more than a couple of hundred people during their entire lives, any more than it is an option today in rural India or among tribal peoples. We now choose whom we will marry, or whether we will marry at all, or live with a friend of the opposite sex (or of the same), or live alone. And whichever of these we choose, we reserve the right to change our minds later! All of our relationships are provisional. And if Christians insist that *their* marriages, at least, aren't provisional, the statistics suggest otherwise. So when we come to consider our relationship with a church, it goes without saying that we are unlikely to be satisfied with anything significantly less than exactly what we want, and even then only for as long as we want it.

Identifying this characteristic in ourselves is the easy part; dealing with it is much harder. What will we do? Castigate it? We have tried and it isn't working. Give up and live with it? That, surely, would be capitulating to the enemy. Or how about a third way? How about asking some fundamental questions concerning what we mean by 'church', and then adjusting ourselves to cope with a social phenomenon that shows no sign of going away?

2

The Meeting Syndrome

Christian churches of all kinds, of course, major on 'preaching up' commitment: to our marriages, to our friendships, to Christ and (by no means least) commitment to those churches. Commitment is the common currency of many of our more 'spiritual' conversations among ourselves. Nevertheless, the fact remains that, in the cultural climate of the late twentieth-century West, our commitment to one another is very low indeed. To be sure, the felt emotional temperature of that 'commitment' may sometimes be very high, but the facts of constantly fragmenting relationships, especially with churches and the people in them, demonstrate that our emotions are a poor guide to its depth.

And the problem is getting worse, not better. For our culture is moving into overdrive. More and more of us live in places very far from where we were brought up, and will move again just as soon as a better job materialises. The executive classes showed us the way during the years after the Second World War and, since theirs was the lifestyle to emulate, more and more of us have followed. Attachment to place and community have given way to choice and opportunity.

The two authors of this book are prime cases in point. We have been friends for a very long time: nearly twenty years. But whereas Chris is one of Meic's oldest friends, the converse is not true. While all sorts of individual accidents and factors of temperament might have come into play in this fact, the overwhelming reason for the difference is a simple sociological one. Chris was born and brought up in a relatively traditional community where few people moved away. Like many others, he studied in the same city, and his biggest move has been to the other side of town. Consequently many of his childhood friends are still around. Meic, by contrast, was brought up in a dormitory suburb where anonymity was taken for granted. Almost none of his schoolfriends would live in the same place now, and neither does he. Consequently none of his friendships go back much more than twenty years, and few as far as that. Furthermore, since we became friends, it is Meic who has moved on. And whereas Chris has left one church in his time, Meic has left several. Even if most of those were for reasons of geographical relocation, the fact remains that relationships have been broken or drastically reduced on the basis of a decision made by him. Is Chris a (relative) stick-in-the-mud? Is Meic disloyal? Whatever his feelings or emotions, it is Meic who, whether or not he likes it or cares to admit it, 'travels light' in terms of relationships. He has to. More and more of us are the same – our life-styles demand it.

And the process is speeding up. We have long been

used to people circulating around the churches in a vicinity. Now, as we are seeing, some Christians are 'spinning out' of the circle altogether. Significant numbers of people who would consider themselves – and be considered by others – 'pretty committed' as Christians, nevertheless cannot commit themselves to a specific local congregation, usually because, in their own minds at least, they cannot stomach the culture of its meetings.

It is not as if churches have been unaware of this development, or as if they have made no attempts to counteract its effects. Many have sought to recreate the kind of community which, in the world outside, is palpably falling apart. If Christians could achieve this, we have reasoned, we would be doing something that is good for its own sake and also a real witness to a fragmented society. Accordingly, many churches have had a tendency to multiply the number of meetings they hold, often to organise some particular project or activity, but often too with the implicit or explicit intention of deepening the members' sense of commitment to one another.

Certainly there is no doubt that participating together in meaningful activities to achieve a particular goal frequently does have this effect. Housegroups are perhaps a prime example of a form of meeting that has become typical of many churches, and for which the explicit aim has been to deepen fellowship and thus 'bonding'. It is also true that they have not generally had the desired effect, mostly because they are sensed by their participants to be artificial communities with no concrete purpose beyond the 'bonding' process itself. (In the same way, marriages in past centuries were relatively strong, in part because they were activity-centred economic units of production. Now that people 'go *out* to work', so that marriages are mainly centres of consumption, relaxation and emotional support, they have become much more fragile.) It may well be that the more meetings are directed towards common action, rather than just *being* together, the more commitment is generated.

Whatever the shortcomings of most housegroups, they have been at least partially successful in creating a sense of community in our churches. At their best, they have brought us together as individuals, given us space to open up to one another, opportunity to share our own experiences and insights into Scripture, to be corrected by others in a secure and friendly atmosphere. They have provided us with friends and a good support network: the church in microcosm. At least, that has been the ideal. However, this comes at the price of a very high commitment of time, which only a minority of Christians are prepared to pay. Those who are not prepared to put a high proportion of their non-working time into meetings – whether housegroups or other gatherings – have generally found themselves somewhat marginalised within the churches, a fact which can itself foster alienation.

In the late 1970s and early 1980s, members of some of the newer churches were encouraged to live in the same area of town, close to the church's place of meeting. Again, this was a strategy intended to foster a sense of community and commitment, and to counteract the atomising tendency of modern society. But such major

shifts in lifestyle – and moving house was a much bigger
commitment for homeowners than it was for students
and those who had just left college – could usually only
be made to work in a climate in which leaders were
generally given larger amounts of authority over the lives
of their flocks than most Christians were used to giving,
or were willing to submit to. Indeed, it came as part of a
package of what older Christians considered to be
authoritarianism.

Of course, it could also be seen as just one expression
of the radicality of the new churches. For the young
people who made up the bulk of the movement, it was
one more sign of their own all-out discipleship; the
failure of other churches to take the same measures was
a further proof of their compromise and worldliness. But
guess what? The students and immediate post-students
began careers, got married and bought houses, and soon
the 'un-freedom' attached to having to live within a mile
or so of a meeting-hall became as unattractive to them as
it had been to their seniors a decade before. The
authoritarianism of the house churches was increasingly
downplayed, and by the early 1990s had all but disappeared.

The fact is that most people today do not live in 'community' at all; they live their lives in the more fluid
context of 'society'. Such communities as do exist are
voluntary and transitory.[1] Most readers of this book will

---

[1] The title of David Prior's book, *Creating Community* (Scripture Press,
1992), is a good example of the understandable self-consciousness – and
to that extent artificiality – of this intention.

not have lived in their present houses for as much as a decade, and the majority will no longer live in them (many not even in the same town) a decade hence. We go 'out to work', generally some distance from where we live. Businesses in the High Street of our town are seldom passed down any longer from one generation to the next; they open for a few years, perhaps a decade or so, and close, get taken over by a multiple or move to other premises. Our children experience their education, not as part of the local community, but as part of the moving kaleidoscope of the public world. If they don't realise straight away that many of their little friends will move away from the area before ever getting to complete their time at the school they started in, then they learn the facts by observation soon enough – if they don't move away themselves. As one journalist recently remarked, many people do not specifically identify with just one town – or even one region – any more; for an increasing number of us, the pattern of our lives is such that we do not even identify with just one country.

It is a commonplace of Victorian history to observe that nineteenth-century Britain, the first industrialised country, witnessed a mushrooming of societies, charities, political groups, sporting associations – voluntary bodies whose participation is mostly translocal and based upon specialised personal or sectional interests. The rise of clubs and societies was part and parcel of the rise of choice and the breakdown of 'community' as traditionally conceived. Participation in them was participation in the wider stage of the public world, or society as a whole.

Similarly, it is no accident that it is the past 200 years that have witnessed the rise in Western churches of a phenomenon that was never there before: parachurch organisations such as mission societies, Christian radio, Christian bikers' clubs, Youth for Christ, the Anabaptist Network, CARE, Intercessors for Britain. Like the Victorian societies, these are special interest groups that secure a following *within* the Christian community, rather than of the Christian community as a whole. They, too, are an example of one of the many ways in which Christians, like everyone else, instinctively live their lives and pursue their own special interests in the context of society, rather than of their own location.[2] And in general, the more urbanised and cosmopolitan the part of the country a given person lives in, the stronger this tendency is. Local participation is at a premium. Neighbourhood institutions have to sell themselves like any other in an environment in which commitment to place is at rock bottom.

In such a context, the idea that we can create highly committed communities focused on a geographical location – especially ones based around a meeting-hall – is to dream of going back to Merrie England. Most contact between Christians and non-Christians takes place in

---

[2] Worship concerts of the 'Soul Survivor' type also represent, by their very nature as large-scale events which are beyond the resources (and, usually, interest) of ordinary congregations, a move away from church as 'community' and towards the anonymity of the public world. This is not to criticise them in the slightest, of course; it is simply an observation of sociological fact.

work, and so the real potential harvest-field is well away from the (potential) evangelist's home church.

Yet the idea of the locally gathered community exerts a continuing, almost 'religious' appeal upon those (especially full-time congregational leaders and ministers) who wish to maximise the *institutional* prominence and appeal of the church. For many, including our best and most influential leaders, their interests are so completely bound up with maximising the size and influence of public meetings, and the institutional structures which those meetings both demand and support, that it is virtually impossible to conceive of 'church' in any other way. The spread of the gospel and the institutional expansion of ecclesiastical structures seem to be just different ways of expressing the same thing. That is one reason why churches find it so hard to have a vision for evangelism in the workplace, whose harvest of converts will never come to *their* club, whose bottoms will never occupy the seats of *their* meeting-hall.

This is not to accuse all churches of selfishness. Such a charge would obviously be absurd. The fault lies rather with our conception of church as a merely local community and institution. But it does help to explain why our most fruitful avenue of contact with non-Christians under modern circumstances – the workplace – is so underutilised.[3] Local congregations thinking of their own institutional position and size prefer to galvanise

---

[3] Mark Greene, *Thank God it's Monday* (Scripture Union, 1997), is a powerful plea for, and instruction in, evangelism in the workplace.

their members to evangelise in the neighbourhood. Since most of us don't know anyone in our neighbourhoods (we've only lived there a while, and value our privacy like everyone else), we end up evangelising people 'from cold' (i.e. on the basis of little or no previous acquaintance) on doorsteps or in open airs, and then, unsurprisingly, aren't too successful. Where this is not the case, as for example with young mothers at home with their children, evangelism through parent-and-baby groups or at the school gate simply exacerbates our problem of more women in the churches than men!

Most of us are very well aware of all these problems, yet we remain steadfastly addicted to the culture of the church as institution and to its mainstay and primary definition, the meeting. We may fight like ferrets in a sack as to what that meeting should be like and who should be the kingpin running it, but the definition of church that surrounds it remains unquestioned.

So when meetings start to decline, our possible conclusions are limited to two: either people are unfaithful and unspiritual, in which case we start to castigate them, or else something is wrong with the meetings. Both explanations have had their devotees. Those who oppose change, those who have absolutised the cultural norms of 'church' as they have known it and liked it until now will, of course, favour the first theory. The world is becoming ever more godless and, even in the church, the 'love of many is growing cold'. But in the 1970s and 1980s it was increasingly felt, in British churches at least, that the latter theory had greater merit: our meetings simply were no longer culturally relevant. A lot of effort was put into bringing meetings up to date, with the introduction of rock music, informality and repetitive chorus-singing. The charismatic movement had many important theological concerns, but at a sociological level it was also a response to the profound cultural shift brought about by the rise of the rock generation and all of the social attitudes that went with it.

So if the local happy-clappy sessions are no longer hitting the spot, and hi-tech rave-ups can never be more than one-offs (even quite regular one-offs if you insist), where does that leave 'church'? One thing that's starting to happen, of course, is that some of the older leaders who were young and in the vanguard of change in the 1970s and 1980s are now reverting to explanation number one: a godless world and unspiritual Christians. And since the world almost always is godless, and since most Christians really are a lot less spiritual than they ought to be, there will usually be just enough people within the Christian community willing to buy this explanation, so that the alternative – looking at our own institutions and their growing cultural irrelevance – doesn't get considered, or not until so late in the day that 'there ain't no ignoring it any more'. Even when the real issue does finally get addressed, the adjustments are painful and accompanied by infighting and recriminations, as we saw at the time of the last 'culture shift' with the rise of the charismatic movement.

In the meantime, of course, congregations are continuing to split, and individuals are continuing to leave their churches. The level of commitment to institutions and meetings and 'community' is continuing to fall.

Christian leaders are pulling all the levers and the ship still isn't responding. Something has gone wrong.

Right now, the voices urging us to ever greater commitment to more and more meetings – and to the people who lead them – are becoming shriller. It's been a classic knee-jerk evangelical response since time out of mind. When the authority of the Bible was under serious attack by apostate liberals at the beginning of the twentieth century, fundamentalists reacted by producing theories of biblical inspiration more wooden and literalist than the Church Fathers, or the Reformers, or earlier evangelicals had ever countenanced.[4] When sexual morality ceased to be upheld as a social norm, evangelicals pounced on the nuclear family, with the man going out to work and mother staying home to keep house, as the biblical pattern, even though prior to the Industrial Revolution extended families had been prevalent in most societies, and most men and women worked together in and around their own homes.[5] Whenever things go wrong and none of the traditional levers are working, our response is usually to raise the volume level in defence of 'biblical norms', by which we mean, of course, the way things have been for as long

---

[4] See eg, Roger Forster and Paul Marston, *Reason and Faith* (Kingsway, 1989), pp 277–342; J. Pelikan in *The Fundamentalist Phenomenon*, ed. N. Cohen (Eerdmans, 1990), pp 6–9; E.R. Sandeen, *The Roots of Fundamentalism* (University of Chicago Press, 1970), pp 106, 115–31.

[5] See Rodney Clapp, *Families at the Crossroads* (IVP, 1993), for a fuller discussion.

as we can remember (which usually isn't very long at all).

There is an alternative strategy we might consider adopting. We might adapt our church culture and our definitions of church life to meet the challenges of our day. Nothing is sacrosanct about our meetings: their time, their length, their culture, the pattern of their content, who contributes to them. Indeed, to a far greater extent than we have been willing to concede, even their existence is open to question, especially when they begin to frustrate the ends they were intended to promote. This, the most subversive possibility of all, is the very area that we will be examining.

3
Disciples or Churchgoers?

It had been quite a walk – almost twenty-six miles we'd been told – and all in aid of that most worthy of causes even in the 1960s: Oxfam. Yog Jog '68 had left me with a limp and feet festooned with blisters, but I wore my scars with pride and a conscious sense of virtue that at least I had done something to help the less fortunate. Somehow an all-night sponsored walk had given me not only a plastic badge but a tangible sense of achievement . . . until I turned up for the evening service at the local church I attended and was greeted with, 'Missed you in the meeting this morning, brother.'

I'd half expected some sort of question about my absence from the 'Lord's Table' (communion), so I was prepared with my explanation, but to no avail. What I ended up being subjected to was a monologue about the importance of 'not forsaking the assembling of ourselves together'. I was left in no doubt that I had been disobedient by forsaking the meeting. A sponsored charity walk came nowhere near to qualifying as a legitimate reason for not being at the meeting. The primary importance of

41

attending meetings was not open for discussion in the evangelical world of thirty years ago.

Ill-equipped to engage with the society in which we were growing up, the struggle to express the faith that had been nurtured in us became a battle for survival. Many didn't make it and became casualties along the way. What discipleship there had been proved to be inadequate, not simply in terms of what teaching and doctrines had been passed on, but in the very fabric of what discipleship should really be all about. What a pity there had been such a lack of empathy for my blistered feet!

Three decades on, I wonder how much things have really changed as attendance at church meetings, conferences and a whole variety of revival and worship celebrations seems to be regarded as mandatory for someone who is really serious about 'going on with God'. The importance of the large-scale meeting seems quite undiminished in what is regarded as essential to discipleship, often missing the point about the all-important relational dynamic that must go so much further than what is achievable in large gatherings.

The biblical pattern seems clearly evident: discipleship most effectively takes place in a context of relationship. This is precisely the model that Jesus used – an approach that was relational, integrated and empowering.

Relational

Whether they were fishermen or tax collectors, what marked out the way Jesus dealt with his disciples was that he called them to relationship *with him*. What was

of utmost importance was that they were *with him*.
When that was no longer possible they were to remember *him*, not simply recall a teaching or an ethical code.
At the heart of the Christian faith is an encounter with a person, a relational dynamic which changes lives. Quite unconventionally, Jesus *chose* his disciples. Common practice of the day was that the would-be disciple shopped around the various teachers on offer before making a choice. What was adhered to was a teaching. Not so with Jesus, whose call was to follow him and enter into a relationship, not sign up to a new philosophy. Furthermore, these new-found disciples found themselves in relationship with other disciples too, for that seems to have been part of the deal: following Jesus meant living in community with others.

Integrated

For those first disciples, life wasn't neatly compartmentalised into the sacred and the secular. The implications of being followers of Jesus touched everything about their lives. Within the Jewish mindset was an understanding of the inter-relatedness of all things; the cycle of rain and sunshine and the fruitfulness of the ground was all dependent on the grace and mercy of God, and becoming disciples of Jesus didn't change that understanding.

Empowering

Called to give up their lives, they would find life itself. In taking the lowest place, they would find themselves given a seat of honour. The surrendering of control of their own lives would result in them being not only free, but also empowered to live as God wanted them to live. Such an approach to matters of status and power was certainly challenging, even in the world of first-century Palestine.

Sadly, what has passed as discipleship in many contemporary contexts seems to have fallen far short of the working model presented by Jesus. The role and place of public preaching and teaching are explored more fully elsewhere in the pages of this book. At this point we simply want to offer the observation that the prime importance attached to the place of public preaching as the chief means by which believers are discipled is suspect. We believe that it is, and should continue to be, a part of the diet of a well-balanced church, but there are serious health risks involved in making large church meetings the main source of nourishment for the body. Far from empowering Christians to think biblically and to take responsibility for their decisions, preaching often produces a reliance on the power of a particularly gifted orator. (Many's the church which has grown a large congregation based on the preaching abilities of the leader, only to experience a significant decline in numbers once that particular church leader has moved on.)

Speakers love to pass on the 'secrets of living an overcoming life' or to 'entertain' us with this week's inspirational gems to help raise the congregation out of the despondency some of them may feel about what they consider to be the shallowness of their own relationship with God. Frequently the issue is bound up with the fact that their own experience of God doesn't match up to what has been presented by the speaker as the standard to be attained. Mike Yaconelli writes:

> 'Every preacher, every writer, every one of us who communicates, alters and shapes reality. Every moving illustration, every gripping story, every testimony, didn't happen (at least, it didn't happen like the storyteller said it happened). . . I am not suggesting that any of these people are deliberately lying, or even that they are lying at all. . .'

Our own reconstructions of the past – even of our own personal history – can all too easily become a distortion, or a fantasy.

> 'Then, when we compare the flawed reconstruction with our present, that creates an even more serious problem; we believe the distortion and use it to evaluate our present.'[1]

How easy it is to create a fantasy that actually parades as reality and sets the listeners on a pathway to disappointment! We need relationships that challenge and debunk these parodies and discover the joy and the pain, the delight and the cost, of true discipleship.

Susan was a student who had been brought up in a Christian home and found her way to a new church during her time at university. She was relieved to discover that she wasn't the only one to experience some difficulties in hearing God speak in her life. She'd lost count of the number of preachers she'd heard talk so confidently about times when they'd heard God speak to

---

[1] Mike Yaconelli, *The Wittenberg Door* (Dec 86/Jan 87).

them. The platform and the public meeting appeared to be places of certainty, of black-and-white solutions, where to admit to unresolved questions was unthinkable. What a relief it was, then, when she eventually found herself among those with whom the struggles, the doubts and the fear that she was somehow inadequate and especially sinful, could be talked through honestly and openly. The truth was able to set her free in more ways than one!

That real discipleship is set in a relational context is, as we have said, crucial. The dynamic modelled by Jesus is corporate. He was the teacher and his disciples were a team. Even when Jesus selected some to be witnesses of special moments, he chose a group of three: Peter, James and John. Much of the learning that took place among those first disciples happened not only in relationship with Jesus, the rabbi, but also in relationship with the others in the group. It was a place where jealousies and rivalries surfaced, where bold claims were made but promises not kept. It was a place of betrayal too, a place where human weaknesses were all too apparent as this particular band of men began to attempt to get to grips with what it meant to be followers of Jesus.

The business of eating, drinking and living together provided the context in which discipleship took place. Living so close to each other meant that it could not have been a place of pretence for long, as each was constantly faced with the truth about himself and his companions. We are given a few glimpses and insights into such moments in the gospel narratives.

The squabbling between the disciples concerning who

was the greatest among them is just one illustration of the fact that all was not sweetness and light as they grappled with the realities of ambition, self-interest and over-confidence. And it was precisely because they were together that Jesus was able to disciple them. It was during the ordinariness of their lives together that this happened:

> They came to Capernaum. When he was in the house, he asked them, 'What were you arguing about on the road?' But they kept quiet because on the way they had argued about who was the greatest. Sitting down, Jesus called the Twelve and said, 'If anyone wants to be first, he must be the very last, and the servant of all.' (Mk 9:33–35)

And then Jesus did something I imagine none of them would ever forget as he pressed the point home:

> He took a little child and had him stand among them. 'Whoever welcomes one of these little children in my name welcomes me.' (Mk 9:36–37)

And time and again it was during their ordinary, every-day lives that Jesus taught them: during a storm on the lake which turned into a particularly memorable lesson in faith for Peter; an 'unexpected' tax bill – payment on demand – which was settled with a novel catch of fish; time spent with those on the margins of society, when it was made clear that he hadn't come to tickle the fancy of the righteous – he really did seem to have time for 'sinners'. For those first disciples, everyday life – not syn-agogue services – was indeed the context in which they learned about the kingdom of God.

Now, of course, times have changed and the context in which we are considering the issue of discipleship is very different. For most people living in Western society, there is little opportunity to live as closely together as Jesus did with Peter, James, John and the others. Indeed, one of the characteristics of contemporary society is isolation and alienation; both the nature and pace of life seem to be working against developing networks of good relationships. These are challenging times indeed for the church to resist the temptation to become facilitators of large-scale meetings, mega-events and the delusion that these will somehow be a means for transforming society. For at best, big meetings can play only a small part in the process. The emphasis upon revival so evident in many of our churches is welcome, but even that, history suggests, need not lead inevitably to wider social transformation. (And the most recent revivals have a poorer record in that regard than those of the eighteenth and nineteenth centuries.)

There are good indications that we are beginning to respond positively to the new challenges facing us in the new cultural situation. The recent interest in the idea of 'cell churches' has been an encouraging sign that there is indeed a realisation of just how critical is the question of creating relationships capable of fostering grass-roots discipleship. It is certainly our contention that, for the sake of the health of the body, we need to be investing in the formation of cells (and groups of cells) of believers. Perhaps it is most noteworthy that this development is taking place even among Christians who are pioneering church in youth culture, where large-scale events – be they concerts or club nights – are very important.

For some of these people, small group activities are considered to be at the very core of how they operate. Billy Kennedy, one of the leaders of Sublime, a youth church which is a part of the Southampton-based Cornerstone grouping, has been a great advocate of discipleship through small groups led by young people themselves. And it seems to be working! Bristol-based NGM, also involved in church planting in youth culture, run a whole range of highly effective training courses built around the sense of ownership, involvement and relationship encouraged through small groups that run alongside concert-style multi-media events.

Essential to true discipleship is honesty, a quality which the culture of our church meetings can do little to encourage. Only from a place where there is the space to be vulnerable, rather than the expectation to conform or perform, can we hope to grow a community of truth where the values of the kingdom of God are expressed in people's lives. But this kind of vulnerability, by its very nature, can never be a normative 'requirement'; once it is institutionalised, then failure is inevitable. It is not a commodity that can be frozen and canned. Like humility, it cannot long survive public demands to prove itself. True discipleship is about enabling others to work out the truth of their own identity in Christ by knowing and being known.

Barry and Linda, searching for a church in the area to which they had recently moved, decided to attend the mid-week meeting of what they had heard was a 'good

fellowship' down the road. They only went once! Treated
to a session of soul-baring, confession and public repentance, they were told this was what happened most
Wednesday nights. Barry and Linda decided to look elsewhere and were spared the future traumas of the group,
where it was not too long before manipulation, fear and
abuse ran riot. The attempt to institutionalise vulnerability and openness is bound to fail, for without the
reality of trust and acceptance they will remain ideals to
reach for but not realities to be experienced.

Dualism

Thankfully, in recent years, much has been said and
written to challenge the dualism of sacred versus secular
that has characterised the thinking of many Christians.
Even so, mixed messages still abound because of what we
understand as 'church'. Attendance at church meetings,
as in the instance at the beginning of this chapter, can
become something we are required to do for its own sake.
The phrase 'going to church' gives away more than how
you intend to spend the next few hours; there is an understanding implicit in the language which is a long way
from what the first Christians thought of as 'church'.
Clearly, the whole thrust of the New Testament is that
Christians *are* church – eating, sleeping, walking,
talking, at work or at play, in meetings or out of them.
Now although such an understanding would certainly
not be foreign to most contemporary evangelicals, in
practice many Christians continue to be 'churchgoers'! It
is our contention that for too long we have relied on

meetings and the culture that surrounds them to be a substitute (an inadequate one) for the real business of discipleship.

As those who have been involved in leading congregations in worship, we are both painfully aware of the difficulties inherent in handling the expectations that corporate worship is all about singing my favourite songs to thrill and excite me sufficiently so that I can survive until my next fix in a week's time. Devoid of an understanding of the true nature of worship (which Jesus said is bound up in 'spirit' and 'truth') and the place it has in our continuing walk with God, what passes as corporate worship can so easily fail to rise far beyond self-indulgence.

When public meetings become the all-important focus for the congregation's spiritual health, not only does this place a great responsibility upon those who organise and lead, but it also puts great power within their grasp. The subtle, corrupting influence of power has been underestimated by many who have later had to face up to its awful consequences. Fear, guilt, manipulation and control can easily become legitimised weapons in the battle to produce the 'appropriate' fruits in any given congregation, as speakers or worship leaders seek to authenticate their 'ministry'. So alarmingly subtle is the pressure to see the required repentance, faith or manifestations, that the leaders themselves can be unaware of just what means they are employing to achieve the required end result. These means can sometimes bear little resemblance to the way Jesus dealt with others.

Large public meetings are the key to creating and expressing corporate identity, an important aspect of the life of any church. But significant dangers lurk here as the focus can so easily slip and become the passing-on of the norms of that particular church culture. Dress code, language, behaviour and mannerisms are all part-and-parcel of how to fit in. There are times when the way in which larger meetings work seems to exclude rather than include; when rather than expressing our individual distinctives – our unity in our diversity – the meeting becomes an expression of an alien subculture which we must fit into by working hard on ourselves. Too often the judgement is made that, if someone finds it difficult to worship in 'our' sort of meeting, then clearly the problem is with them. The truth might well have more to do with the monocultural expressions of church meetings.

In a society that is increasingly diverse, we continue to be incredibly conservative and, in many ways, sterile in our approach to style and form. We forget that the architecture and decor of our church buildings communicates so much about our values. Often built around the needs of the large gathering, resources can end up being poured into constructing and maintaining buildings that do little to encourage interaction and relationship dynamics. Faced with a straight choice between a pub or restaurant on the one hand, and an average church building on the other, few people would have much of a struggle to decide which looked the more inviting.

Clearly many denominations, groupings and streams have styles and forms of worship, meetings – and the buildings to house them – which are quite distinctive, something which is positively encouraging as our very diversity reflects the hugely creative God we serve. Problems arise, however, when the norms and stylistic features of one particular group or stream are spoken of as definitively expressing 'kingdom culture'. Approaches to what amount to little more than cultural differences must never be mistaken for the truths, principles and values of the kingdom of God which can be expressed in cultures the world over. As the church grapples with issues of diversity (as it must), and as more varied and diverse expressions of church proliferate, the great challenge will be to discover ways in which corporateness can be expressed. The temptation, as always, will be to fragment, to remain within groups of those who do things in a way we are comfortable with, and not to rise to meet the challenge of being church together. Inevitably there will be misunderstanding. For those whose security is in the very structure and form of expression, then to entertain the idea of other Christians 'being church' in a very different way from themselves could be extremely threatening.

In one New Church context, some of the leaders and members of the larger 'parent' congregation began to feel decidedly uncomfortable that the smaller and newer congregation that had been planted out in an adjoining community was developing a distinctive and different flavour. The core values of both groups remained identical, but something fundamental seemed to be threatened by diversity in practice. Failure to resolve this led to a major fracture in relationships, complete with traumas in abundance. It is hardly an uncommon story.

But what a tremendous challenge! That discipleship is critically important we have no doubt. That large church meetings are not the places where the real business is done, we are sure. It is time for an intelligent re-evaluation in the light of Scripture, our experience and the needs of the days in which we live.

4

Culture Wars

One of the main reasons why so many Christians are dissatisfied with the churches that they continue to bless with their presence, is that they dislike the meetings for one reason or another. And a very high proportion of that irritation is with what we can call the 'culture' of the meetings. As often as not, it is the type of music used in worship that causes friction, though in some churches in the past people have fought over whether or not there should be music at all.

Often, Christians express irritation at arrangements in this area with which one might have thought that, broadly, they were in sympathy. Just because a Christian describes themselves as 'charismatic' does not mean that they will be happy with any and every type of worship-style that could be so described. Far from it. Within that category there are infinite variations. Traditional Pentecostal worship of the *Redemption Hymnal* type would leave most young Pentecostals these days seething with frustration. Music that would go down well at New Wine Bible week would strike even some fellow-Anglican charismatics (of the ultra-mellow variety, or the classical music, Praise Proms types) as a little crass. Connoisseurs can even tell at a hearing which worship tape comes from the New Frontiers stable and which from the (to an outsider ostensibly similar, but to an insider very different) Pioneer circle. The same is true of non-charismatics. The liturgy of Anglicans in the Reform stream may be a virtual abomination to devotees of the *Grace Hymnal*. They might differ, too, over whether guitars are permissible, or irreverent and unsuitable, even for playing hymns.

In each case, Christians are expressing a preference which, though it may call itself theological, is primarily cultural. If this seems to be putting this point too strongly, we might at least agree that it is the culture of the meetings about which a preference is being expressed.

Cultural differences emerge, too, over what type of sermon should be given (or whether one should be given at all), how frequently, how long, whether it should always be expounding some particular text of Scripture, or whether it should be thematic. One preacher in a Brethren church was reproved by his hearers on a Sunday evening because he 'didn't preach the gospel', meaning that he had failed to give a sermon of the type which ends with an appeal to any unconverted present (though there seldom were any) to repent and be saved.

Other aspects of meetings are also subject to strong preferences from Christians, and these too relate to the culture of meetings. A large inscription on the front wall proclaiming 'Holiness Unto the Lord' has strong cultural connotations with a particular type of spirituality. No one could disagree with the sentiment it expresses but, for their very different reasons, Grace Baptists and trendy charismatics would be left feeling a little uneasy about it. A square formation of chairs around a table makes one kind of cultural statement about the meeting; straight rows facing a large fixed and raised pulpit make a different statement. And slightly curved rows facing a slightly raised platform indicate a compromise! A building with a large internal balcony indicates a very different sort of meeting – and so a different sort of meeting culture – to one with a single carpeted floor and no pillars.

Most Christians are, in fact, very particular indeed about just what kind of meeting-culture they like. Though most of them will tolerate deviation from their preference on an occasional basis (variety is almost always refreshing), most know exactly what they want by way of regular fare, and express annoyance when they don't get it, or when their own preference changes and the congregation fails to adjust with them.

The fact is that every public meeting takes place on the basis of a particular culture. And so the inevitable question arises: Whose? Will it be the culture that you like, or the one that I like? Will it be the kind that makes introverts feel comfortable and is implicitly disdainful of expressive types, or one that gives extroverts maximum scope for their extroversions and frowns on those of quiet dispositions for somehow not being 'free in the Lord'? Will it be on the basis of the attitudes of your generation, or of mine? Of your social class, or of mine?

Of your ethnic background, or of mine? Even if the culture of the meeting is in fact a compromise (as most are), it still needs to be negotiated, not just once, but on an ongoing basis. And therein, of course, lies the foundation of so many of our conflicts with one another.

My generation or yours?

Charismatic issues were at the heart of the upheavals in many churches of the 1970s and early 1980s. In many instances, the call for the freedom of *charismata* was the call for greater congregational participation in meetings. But these demands were themselves strongly connected with the cultural differences between generations, and so tended to focus upon worship-styles. Formally, the battle-lines were drawn up over theological propositions about the continuance of tongues and prophecy in the post-apostolic church. In point of fact, however, any casual visitor to a church could tell where a church stood by reference to its musical – and therefore its cultural – arrangements.

Many older people insisted that the worship music of the rock generation was in fact irreverent, and the authors remember how the hymns of Sankey's *Sacred Songs and Solos* were defended as being timeless expressions of *true* godliness, unlike the ephemeral trash of the guitar players. This hymnbook had been popularised in the late nineteenth century as a result of the evangelism of American evangelist Dwight Moody, with his solo-singer, Ira Sankey. However, the late nineteenth century lasted well into the 1970s in

South Wales chapels, and replacing the 'sacred' book and the culture which its songs embodied was an uphill struggle.

The irony is, of course, that these hymns – and their near contemporaries in the *Redemption Hymnal* – had themselves been rejected in the 1880–1920 period by older Christians of that time, on precisely the same grounds that were later to be used to defend them against the encroachment of modern choruses and rock music. The songs of the Holiness movement and the early Pentecostals were thought to be demeaning because they deliberately copied the secular music-hall style of the turn of the century. The solos – and even some of the hymns – in Sankey's collection were considered demeaning to the gospel because, it was alleged, they showed a ghastly sentimentality. And, of course, they did. But then so did the secular songs of that time (think of 'Sonny boy', or of literary characters like Tiny Tim or the Little Match-Girl). Gross sentimentality was all the rage in the Victorian period – it scratched where people were itching. So the Christians who opposed Sankey's hymns in the 1880s were wrong, just as those who defended them in the 1970s as if they were some kind of God-given absolute were also wrong.

The despisers of Sankey and the music-hall style in the late nineteenth century could look back to the great hymns of Charles Wesley over 100 years before. Why, oh why didn't anyone write hymns like that any more? *There* was songwriting that really reflected the power of conversion and the majesty of the gospel! The trouble is that Wesley's hymns had also been decried in *his* day as so much demeaning doggerel designed to accompany the nasty populist emotionalism of the early Methodist awakenings. At that time, nonconformists had been among the early Methodists' chief critics. Why, they had asked, couldn't the likes of Charles Wesley write *good* hymns, like the Congregationalist Isaac Watts of the previous generation?

But Watts had had to overcome the objections of diehards of the early eighteenth century for encouraging the elect and the unregenerate to sing words which were appropriate only to the former, thus affronting the majesty of God, and for encouraging women to sing in church, when Scripture said that they should be silent![1] True godliness should be observed by sticking to the strictly biblical language of the Calvinist metrical psalms of earlier generations . . . which in turn had been vilified in their day as 'Geneva jigs'!

The same thing is true of the language of religious worship. The King James Version of the Bible has been defended as the only permissible translation: 'People have died for the King James Bible,' as a friend of ours was told. While this is untrue, if we accept the point that people certainly *did* die for the Tyndale version upon which it was based, that was because the martyrs were determined to have the Scriptures in a language that people could understand. Were they alive today, they would be the first to insist that we use modern translations! For the defenders of the 'AV' or 'KJV', however, seventeenth-century English has become another sacred

---

[1] M. Watts, *The Dissenters*, vol 1 (OUP, 1978), pp 308–12.

language – like Latin before it – to which all people who come after it must be bound.

Similarly, the 1662 *Book of Common Prayer* has been defended as if it were somehow inherently sacred, whereas it was a revision of Cranmer's prayer books of 1549 and 1552, which were first put together to help make the liturgy of the Church of England intelligible to ordinary people. The idea was to liberate them from being bound to Latin, which they did not understand but which was considered by many at the time to be specially sacred. The same thing has happened with the liturgy of the Eastern churches. Methodius and Cyril, who were ninth-century missionaries to the Slavs, created the Glagolitic alphabet (upon which the later Cyrillic alphabet was based). They also composed a liturgy for the Slavic churches in a language, which came to be called Church Slavonic, that the worshippers could comprehend. Time has moved on and language has changed. Church Slavonic is no longer comprehensible to ordinary churchgoers, but by now it is a hallowed language which, some insist, cannot be tampered with. As Maggi Dawn comments, 'Sometimes you have to change to stay the same.'[2] But that is something we are very good at finding spiritual reasons for not doing.

At the risk of labouring the point, it should by now be clear that every change in the culture of worship has been attacked as somehow inherently ungodly, in the name of some supposedly absolute tradition of true godliness,

---

[2] M. Dawn in *The Post-evangelical Debate*, G. Cray *et al.*, (SPCK, 1997), pp 35–56.

which upon examination turns out to be simply the innovation of a previous generation. In each case, what has been absolutised is not the gospel, but a particular cultural expression of the gospel. The authors for their own part are not lovers of rap music, but, hey, we're in our forties! If we thought about it, we could certainly come up with some spiritual-sounding reasons why it should never be employed in worship meetings, but such 'reasons' would be, in fact, simply rationalisations for absolutising our own cultural preferences and denouncing those of younger people.

Gerald Coates has pointed out the same tendency in respect of attitudes towards television. During the 1950s, when TV sets started entering the homes of most of the population, many evangelicals denounced them as worldly. After all, they were even advertised as 'bringing *the world* into your living room'! By the late 1960s, even traditionally-minded Christians had succumbed to the charms of the flickering box, but colour TVs were being introduced, so it was these which were now worldly, while black and white was OK. By the early 1980s, videos were just coming in and everyone had moved over to colour, so it was videos which were now worldly! As Gerald pointed out, the way to be truly spiritual was always, apparently, to be at least fifteen years out of date!

The dramatic rise of the charismatic and house churches in the 1970s and 1980s, following their origins over the previous decades, saw the churches' most recent painful adjustment to the new cultural realities. But as time has passed, making even these somewhat *passé*, and as the generation gap has widened yet further, we are now witnessing the rise of youth churches, whose ranks are filled by young Christians impatient with the failure of their own congregations to 'meet their needs' or express their cultural preferences. As before, their very existence is provoking the righteous indignation of those who are quick to point out that the body of Christ should include all generations, social backgrounds and races etc. One wonders: are such protests a promise by those who make them that their congregations will make themselves more appealing to young people? (And if they do, how will the old feel about it?) Or is it just a demand that the young stay where they are, put up and shut up?

Our point is that there are no sensible, non-incriminating answers to these questions. There are no justifications – on either side – that are not easily unmasked as self-serving rationalisations. The demand for 'unity' centred around large meetings is the demand that somebody's culture be subsumed or dominated by somebody else's . . . as part and parcel of acceptance of the gospel.

My class or yours?

The same thing is true in respect of social background, or what used to be called 'class'. The churches and non-conformist chapels of the nineteenth century were increasingly unacceptable to the urban poor, a fact dramatically highlighted by the religious census of 1851, which showed that, on a given Sunday, only 50 per cent of the population attended any sort of church or chapel and, of those who did, only half attended their parish (i.e. Anglican) churches. Attendance rates were lowest in the big cities like London and Liverpool, especially in those areas where the poor were concentrated. The culture of the churches – of all types – simply repelled them. They could not afford the fine clothes that appeared to be necessary to attend. They could not afford pew rents. The values of order and hierarchy which most churches exuded held no appeal for those at the bottom of the existing order of things. The denomination which was most successful in reaching the poor – the Primitive Methodists – had a meeting culture (plenty of emotion, few full-time clergy and, until the mid-century, no training colleges) which was much more amenable and accessible to them. By contrast, the Congregationalists at that time were perhaps the most middle-class denomination of all, with impressive buildings, learned preachers and intellectually demanding sermons.[3] The difference between the two denominations was as much cultural as theological. Each would have felt out of place in the meetings of the other. But even the Primitive Methodists had their limits, and were slowly becoming more bourgeois. The Salvation Army was started in the 1860s as a way of reaching the poorest of the poor. The culture of the other churches was simply so alien to such people that they could not have been reached by them.

The early Pentecostals took much of their ethos from the Primitive Methodists and Salvationists. It was for

---

[3] D. Bebbington, *Evangelicalism in Modern Britain* (Unwin Hyman, 1989), pp 110–4; O. Chadwick, *The Secularization of the European Mind in the Nineteenth Century* (CUP, 1975), pp 88–106; M. Watts, *The Dissenters*, vol 2 (OUP, 1995), pp 22–9, 303–27, 682–870.

these reasons, as much as any other, that many middle-class Christians found them so repulsive. Shouting and ranting and singing repetitive music-hall-style choruses in a tin tabernacle was simply not dignified! When the charismatic movement in the denominations began in the 1950s and 1960s, it was a far more middle-class affair. When its first magazine, *Trinity*, began publication, it 'made no place for merely Pentecostal news' and events.[4] The reason? Respectability, of course!

In our own time, the middle-classness of most churches, quite apart from any generational factors, remains a problem in evangelising the poor. The Jesus Army has been easily the most successful organisation in appealing to the very poorest. Indeed, it is precisely those alleged factors about the Jesus Army which caused great controversy within the evangelical community (in the 1980s, at least) – authoritarianism, military style, an arguably simplistic biblicism, sharing of homes and property – which have permitted them to have the greatest impact among people who have fewer freely made choices or material goods to give up, and who never placed such a high value in the first place upon 'thinking for themselves' as do those who have obtained their 'A' Levels. At the other end of the spectrum, several of the Anglican churches in London have found a constituency among the hyper-prosperous.

To a lesser extent than with generational differences, but unmistakably nevertheless, class differences are reflected in our public meetings, and will both repel and

---

[4] P. Hocken, *Streams of Renewal* (Paternoster, 1986), p 184.

attract on that basis. Whatever their merits or demerits, it is a fairly safe bet that the Praise Proms type of Christians will never have anything to say to high-rise dwellers in New Cross, and whatever the strengths of their biblical arguments, the gains of the Jesus Army in Gerrard's Cross are likely to be strictly limited. What is expected to be said, or the type of emphasis that is made about behaviour, or the assumptions about members' circumstances, or what they are expected to understand or know about, or what they will like to sing – all of these things shape the culture of a meeting. If they are 'wrong' for a given individual, then they are likely to feel out of place, or irritated, or frustrated, especially in the long term. As a result, some churches are generally working class – with exceptions – while rather more are middle class – with exceptions – in their ethos and the culture of their meetings. This is fine, and in many ways inevitable, but again we need to beware of self-righteously absolutising the culture of 'our' social background as somehow being normative, and stigmatising others as some kind of deviant separatists.

My tribe or yours?

The same point can be made, obviously, about ethnic background. Most white churches were a lot less than fully hospitable to black immigrants in the period after the Second World War. A lot of this was plain, sinful racism. Nevertheless, it has to be admitted that many of the black churches which have sprung up are more than simply refuges from white prejudice. To an extent, at

least, they reflect distinctive ethnic cultural characteristics which could not receive their full expression in
more multicultural churches. If they were to come
together – as perhaps they should – with white churches,
how much expression should that cultural difference be
given in meetings? And how would agreement be reached
as to what was too much, or not enough? And what
would those who dissented from such decisions do?
Again, our point is that agreement is unlikely or impossible, and that 'unity' could only be achieved by suppres-
sion of identity in a homogenised mass.

As with music, as with generational and social differences, unity (or something approaching unity) *is* possible, but only where 'the meeting' is not central to 'being
church', for where it is, it is inevitable that those meetings
simply become the battleground for cultural expression:
Whose music? Whose format? Whose mode of discourse?

Perhaps this issue is most clearly seen in what we might
call 'the Caernarfonshire question'. North-west Wales is
badly underevangelised. It is an overwhelmingly Welsh-
speaking area, with a great past of revivals and lively
churches and a deathly present of liberal and dying ones.
The Welsh chapels became the bastions of the language
against the flood of Anglicisation over the past 150 years
and, although much of what remains is due to their
efforts, in the process, they have become merely cultural,
and no longer spiritual, centres. Such evangelical
churches as exist in this area are of two types. In the first
place are a small number of Welsh-speaking churches
which adhere quite rigidly to the cultural patterns of the

past. Not only in doctrine, but in hymnody, preaching style and total mode of discourse, they attempt to be 'faithful', as they see it, to the legacy of the great days of evangelicalism in rural Wales. In doing so, they have absolutised the culture of an age that is long gone, and made it, in effect, a part of the gospel, acceptance of which is necessary to inclusion within their ranks.

In the second place are the churches of the English incomers. Many or most of these are charismatic and, to a far greater extent, 'up to date'. They have been through and accepted the culture shift that hit the English-speaking churches in the 1970s and 1980s. But there is a major drawback: they speak English. To be fair, some of these churches make faint attempts to be bi-lingual, but without profound efforts at cultural identification (i.e. really 'going native' and learning the language properly), this can never succeed. If there are ten people in the room and nine of them can speak Welsh, the language of their discourse will be English. (Otherwise, the tenth person will tell himself – and anyone else who will listen – that all of the others were really saying insulting things about him to one another.) Since Welsh speakers can all speak good English, and the English speakers don't usually learn Welsh, the loser in this situation is preordained. As a result, the English-speaking churches have almost no impact on the Welsh-speaking population, who realise that surrender of their language and culture is, in effect, part of the 'gospel' which they are being offered.

At this point, some of the English speakers frequently protest that language is being made more important than the gospel. And, of course, it is: *their* English language, since they refuse – or, at any rate, fail – to offer the gospel in the language of the natives! In the meantime, Caernarfonshire remains unevangelised, since both types of church are culturally irrelevant. One has absolutised the culture of a past to which contemporaries – and especially young people – cannot relate, while the other has absolutised their own, alien language, with the result that anything they might say is simply 'screened out' by the majority of the target audience who see them as simply one more part of the Anglo threat to their entire way of life.

This issue highlights, in the most dramatic way, the case we have been making. If a meeting is held, in whose language will it be? On the basis of whose culture will it be? If it is not on the basis of mine, then I am unlikely to give it a hearing if I am a non-Christian, and it is unlikely to have more than the shakiest hold on my allegiance even if I am a Christian. Especially not in a society in which I have so much choice.

Whose unity?

All of this flies in the face of the conventional wisdom of all churches that unity is to be maintained at all costs – even though our history, both ancient and recent, is in the opposite direction. Has not Jesus prayed 'that they may be one'? Of course, unity is an important virtue, but it cannot be achieved on the basis of subsumption of identity. At any rate, it is not *being* achieved on that basis. That is the message being given by the masses of people who are constantly changing churches, leaving them, or creating splits and breakaways. However, we contend that it is the centrality to 'being church' of the large meeting which threatens subsumption and constantly provokes protest, conflict and friction. No meeting of any size and regularity can take place without a 'culture', explicit or implicit, and that leaves those who dissent from the culture of the meeting, for good reasons or bad (or just for understandable reasons), creating trouble.[5] And in a society in flux, increasingly multicultural, with constantly widening generation gaps and a burgeoning of personal choice, there will always be a fertile supply of dissenters of one kind or another. The practice of 'church' in which a large-scale regular meeting is the central feature will not bring us together. Increasingly, it is pulling us further and further apart.

And always, it seems, the loudest cries in favour of 'unity', or 'the authority of the leaders' (or of the denomination, or organisation) come from those who calculate, either openly or tacitly, that *theirs* will be the culture that dominates the 'united' group. It is the middle-aged who are outraged at youth churches, the whites who are suspicious of black separatism, the Anglo-Christians in North Wales who huff that language is being made more important than the gospel. One might protest that these voices are masks for oppression but, frankly, such protest is hardly necessary. Quite

---

[5] L. Singlehurst, *Sowing, Reaping, Keeping* (Crossway, 1995), pp 88–95, recognises that cultural and generational differences are among the biggest hindrances to evangelism and to integrating converts into the life of existing churches.

simply, they are being listened to less and less. If their moral blandishments are heeded, they will indeed keep some people in unwilling subjection for a while longer. If they are not heeded, there will be a new wave of secessions and splits, or acrimonious revolutions within congregations that then leave supporters of the *status quo ante* feeling trodden upon. And after that, a little way up the road, the process will repeat itself all over again over another set of issues.

There is an alternative. We could push aside the centrality of the big meeting and find another way to 'be church'. Together.

5
Keeping the Engine Running

The power and the glory?

Intrigue, deception and rivalries. Infighting, factions and betrayal. It's not just the stuff of the latest television dramas, but alarmingly close to what goes on behind the scenes in many churches. You wouldn't have to search very hard to come across some fairly juicy gossip about a church near you! Spiritualise the language and what many churches experience is little different from the cut and thrust of boardroom politics with its struggles for power and control. Of course, the terminology is very different, and motives are heavily disguised, even to the point at which those who are the key players are not always aware of exactly what is going on themselves. Sometimes out of what we feel to be the most sincere of motives we can end up serving ourselves and our own egos rather than God.

Having clocked up the best part of fifty years' experience of church life between us, and knowing churches across the country in a wide variety of denominations and groupings, we've learned that the rhetoric of platforms and the good intentions of end-of-meeting commitments often do not hold up when the pressure is on. Often characterised by splits and fractured relationships, it seems we regularly fall short of the sort of unity Jesus prayed for so passionately just before the cross.

Someone in church leadership commented recently that in his church, due to recent difficulties, people had come to associate the word 'vision' with trouble. It had been 'strength of vision' that had led to a major division in the church. The movers and shakers found themselves with differing ideas about the way forward, priorities and 'God's strategy'. To many observers, the central issue was one of power, but that was a difficult one for the main players in this particular drama to recognise in themselves. Lord Acton's dictum about the corrupting effects of power needs to be taken very seriously indeed. Dressed in religious clothes, it seems even more subtle and difficult to recognise for what it is – especially when it appears within ourselves.

For many of us, power doesn't become an issue until we perceive our own area of control to be challenged or our power-base threatened. For those who exercise control in a given situation (say, running a church meeting or an aspect of it), the prospect of losing that can cause us to question our very identity, which so often becomes bound up in what we do. For those who step out of leadership for whatever reason, there is a period of adjustment and often a sense of loss.

Hilary had been in local church leadership for a number of years but demands of work and family made it increasingly difficult for her to function well. Despite having become involved in new initiatives in the church, she was clearly under pressure and not coping. The other leaders, seeing what was happening, were mindful of Hilary, her family and the church. They suggested that she took time out of the leadership team, a decision to which both Hilary and her husband agreed. But things were not as straightforward as they appeared to be. The couple acknowledged their circumstances were difficult, but began to be suspicious of the motives of the other leaders. Did they just want them out of the way? Would Hilary ever be allowed to return? What would others in the church think? What would they do now?

Things did not go well and it soon became obvious that, although Hilary had more time for work and family, there was something of a crisis of identity too. She began to find it increasingly difficult to remain in the church until eventually the whole family moved away and Hilary became part of the leadership team of another church. Undoubtedly there were other factors involved but, to those close to the situation, one of the major issues did seem to be that of position and power. The roles we play – and are seen to play in meetings – and the way we are thought of by others as a result become critically important to how we view ourselves.

We've recently heard some New Church leaders comment on how few younger people in their circles seem to be entrusted with any significant responsibility. This seems particularly disappointing, as many of today's New Church hierarchy were in leadership themselves while relatively young. Does the church become a power-base which it is difficult to let go? Where does the pursuit of one's calling and the exercise of a God-given ministry stop and the need for recognition, worth and identity start? It's been good to see recent efforts by the Evangelical Alliance to begin to tackle the need for young leaders, but the church must be one of the few places where you can still be regarded as a young leader until well into your forties!

In a number of situations it would be difficult for a younger person or a newcomer to have much of a shaping influence because any attempt to get involved could be seen as a threat to personal fiefdoms, whether in worship groups, ladies' meetings or missionary prayer groups. All sorts of meetings – the main church gatherings on Sundays (where it's usually highest level leadership who get to run things) and smaller midweek events (the most likely place for 'ordinary' types to be allowed some responsibility) – can be breeding grounds for the urge to control. In most instances, these activities may have begun out of sincere motives and for clear purposes, but only continue (sometimes after they have outlived their usefulness, or in extreme cases even their viability) because they have become somebody's power-base. And this is certainly not a situation exclusive to more traditional churches. Some ministers have been shocked at the resistance they have encountered as they have talked of changing the structure or place of meetings. There have been times in our experience when the suggestion to change the style or approach of a meeting has certainly felt like touching the proverbial sacred cow.

Maybe the very structure of a given meeting – the time, place and format – can become a great source of security in itself. It certainly can and does become a significant factor in influencing a congregation whose expectations are often shaped by the Sunday meeting experience. It is usually a powerful means whereby the core values of a church will be communicated and re-enforced, and this happens through everything that happens, not just the sermon. From how people are dressed to the language they use, from the style of the music to the seating arrangements and the extent to which ordinary members are free to participate – all of these things will communicate the values of that particular church.

At an extreme, of course, there are some churches where the power-base is almost unassailable and to question decisions made by the leaders would be tantamount to questioning God himself. But even at a more moderate level, observing the differences between churches can be . . . well, enlightening. During recent changes in how two relatively large churches organised themselves, it was interesting to note the very different approaches taken to change by the leaders.

The first church decided on a gradualist approach that took about twelve months in all. Following a number of open church days, the leaders set up a series of Saturday workshops and training sessions for anyone interested in getting to know more about the thinking behind the alterations that the leaders were proposing. There was every opportunity to question, to get clarification and time to consider the implications of the new structure. The leaders were keen to take the church with them and to make the process as inclusive as possible.

The second church effected the same change in a far shorter period of time: it was announced that the leaders had decided that God was telling them to change, so from next week things would be different! The explanation went something like this: there was no opportunity for wider discussion because leaders led. They had heard from God, and if any of the members didn't agree, then obviously they didn't trust the leaders . . . which was a fair indication that such members were probably in the wrong church!

Frequently churches – or power-bases within them – become locked into being controlled by the members of one or two families. There are few places with stronger family networks, sometimes spanning many generations, than a longstanding local church! Of course, this behaviour is entirely understandable, but it remains wrong. It is also self-defeating if the church truly wishes to grow and allow new people to really feel included, as opposed to just saying that it aspires to these things.

Not surprisingly, those who feel 'locked out' of real involvement in existing structures and meetings tend to seize the opportunity to get involved in new initiatives. It may well be that the thought of being part of a new church plant does genuinely excite and inspire people, but experience seems to suggest that there can also be other, less virtuous motives at work. Few situations seem to cause quite as much unrest as the recognition of leadership in a new project or church plant. Having witnessed and been part of a few such situations, it is often startling to observe just what emerges in this virgin territory. Undoubtedly, much of what happens could be due to feelings of frustration that have been building up at the home base for some of the reasons we have alluded to: for example, there simply isn't the space or opportunity to help shape the future. It's possible that the existing leadership structure has produced a bottleneck and there is a genuine need to create space and opportunity for others to take on responsibility.

Unfortunately there are also occasions when, for some, the new venture presents the opportunity to seek power because of what they have learned to think of as success. The hierarchical structure practised and perpetuated by much within church culture models a pattern that is more clearly based on worldly principles than on a biblical understanding of the servant nature of leadership which Jesus taught, and of which he provided a living example. Many times Jesus taught on this theme, giving advice about those who wished to be first needing to make themselves last. Those who sought to be the greatest were told they should become the servants of all. And the supreme example of that, of course, is the cross itself.

The choice Jesus made when he went to the cross 'did something to power itself – it redeemed it. . . . If redemption has to reach as far as sin has gone, and if power has been corrupted by the fall, then power itself has been one of the objects of redemption.' The nature of redeemed power and one of the characteristics that saves it from having a corrupting influence on those who wield it is that it has 'a radically different orientation, it is wholly for others, not power for self nor power over others'.[1]

---

[1] Tom Marshall, *Understanding Leadership* (Sovereign World, 1991), pp 63–5.

'The Lost Generation'?

We have already noted the age profile of those who hold and exercise power in churches. At a recent leaders' meeting, one 'successful' pastor responded to a question about young leaders with the comment that, as he had been made to wait until his forties before being given a position of authority, he felt it only right that the current generation should also have to wait. He certainly wasn't prepared to think of those in their twenties and thirties as fellow leaders. The whole issue of younger men and women leading is interesting, for there is often a significant gap between our theory and our practice. What is spoken in terms of encouragement to the young is often not followed through in what is entrusted to them. Even some of those committed to working specifically with young people seem reluctant to allow them the opportunity to pioneer a new way; the place of power is a difficult one to give up.

So we can have a situation in which God's calling on someone is clearly recognised and widely agreed with, but because he or she is young and likely to challenge the *status quo*, there is much concern about actually giving that person the space to do something. Mostly this concern is expressed in a form that is hard to argue with: after all, which young person has had sufficient life experience or a level of maturity that is beyond question?

The real (albeit implicit) issue in seeing younger people brought into church leadership strikes directly at the heart of the issue of power and vested interest. The fear of allowing the young to take things on is in the

KEEPING THE ENGINE RUNNING

knowledge that they are unlikely to do it the way we did
(unless, of course, we've managed to produce clones
rather than disciples), and our responses to that fear may
reveal where our security really is.

The issue of how much space and opportunity to
allow the young is one that has been and undoubtedly
will continue to be hotly debated in many churches.
Much has been said in recent times about a coming move
of God among young people. The church in the UK certainly needs to experience something dynamic in relation
to young people, for statistics seem to suggest that
numerically we are losing the fight. The recent Welsh
Churches Survey presented sobering reading indeed for
churches within the Principality. In relation to the
general population, only 4% of 20- to 29-year-olds are a
part of a church, and the figures for 0- to 14- and 15- to
19-year-olds are only slightly higher at 8% and 6%
respectively. Figures available for other parts of the UK
do not paint a very different picture.

For John Gallacher, the compiler of the survey in
Wales, 'The central issue is one of cultural relevance and
the cost is our church subculture rather than our theology . . . our culture is a vehicle for our spirituality, not its
origin. Church cultures come and go, none are pre-
scriptive, none are normative and none are sacrosanct.
All give way after they have had their time. The only
question is when.'[2] A joint report by the Evangelical
Alliance and the Evangelical Missionary Alliance comes
to similar conclusions: the *Friends* generation of

---

[2] *Challenge to Change*, Results of the Welsh Churches Survey.

twenties and thirties is abandoning our meetings, leaving
the prospect of 'the church of tomorrow becoming even
less accessible to those outside of it'. Those churches that
do buck the trend, however, do so through 'social events,
meals, marriage preparation courses and small group
meetings in people's homes'. Sunday evening services
and mid-week prayer meetings were the most unpopular
with this age group. John Earwicker summed up the
urgent priorities: 'We want to encourage more churches
to develop relational approaches to evangelism.'[3]

Sometimes our apparent reluctance to provide younger
leaders with the opportunity and space that will allow
them to run with what God has given them smacks of
arrogance. One of the key players in the last major revival
in mainland Britain was a 25-year-old Welsh miner, Evan
Roberts, supported by half a dozen or so helpers mainly
in their late teens or early twenties. Spurgeon – admittedly an extreme case – was given space to begin his
preaching career at the age of sixteen and was a pastor at
seventeen. By his early twenties he was one of the most
influential preachers in England! Being misunderstood,
misrepresented and disapproved of seems to be a
common experience of many younger Christians who are
passionate to experience and communicate a Christian
faith that is relevant and effective in their world. Naïvety,
immaturity, idealism and lack of experience don't dis-
qualify them as far as God is concerned.

David was a young man who had an obvious enthusiasm for God. His local church had been pleased to

---

[3] *New Christian Herald*, 2nd May 1998.

support him while he undertook a year's training in leadership and evangelism with a national network of churches. Committed to working with his home church, he turned down the offer of a university place elsewhere in the UK and enrolled on a second-choice course near to home. The next few years went well and he was a great catalyst and enthuser. God really had seemed to have marked him out in some way and time after time conference speakers would pray and prophesy over him, singling him out of hundreds and sometimes thousands of others. But back at base all did not go smoothly as some began to voice their concern about character weaknesses. Without a doubt, David did have much that he needed to work on, but the force and weight of the objections became debilitating and crushing until David eventually caved in under the pressure. Disillusioned, he walked away from the faith altogether. Had the expectations of him been unrealistic? Were the character weaknesses real? Did the radical nature of his understanding of how church might be for his generation rock the boat too much? Was his gifting a challenge to the power structures of his home church?

There are occasions when some of us can hold on to power because we mistakenly perceive this to be the only way to validate the past: only we can be trusted to perpetuate it faithfully into the future. Yet the irony is that, in the fight to hold on, what is often perpetuated is the form, structure and pattern, rather than the life itself. For one of the writers who spent his early years in a Brethren church, the outworking of this tendency has been painfully obvious. What began as a fresh and dynamic move of the Holy Spirit in the last century has, in many places, been reduced to a faithful remnant holding on to a form that has little to do with the original vision. Power has remained with, and will in many instances die with, the Establishment.

Friends first?

Church as an objectified entity, of course, is bound to carry with it considerable baggage. Some of this is inevitable as the logistics of organising large numbers of people necessitate structure. Yet there seems to be an irresistible temptation to become bound by, and to end up serving, the very structures originally set in place to contain and channel life. Meetings themselves often continue year after year simply because they always have done, with few questions asked about the relevance and effectiveness of what they contribute to the life of the church. That is because, for most of us, meetings are the life of the church! Stripped of the formalised timetable of the usual range of weekly meetings, many churches would simply cease to exist.

If this really were to happen, however, new expressions of friendship might well emerge, and new ways of relating together as church. Churches that have gone through periods of persecution, when they have been unable to meet formally, have often reported a tremendous sense of renewal and a greater depth in their relationships. Such levels are often lost once 'normality' returns and the weekly timetable can safely be reinstated.

Surely if we are to be a truly incarnational church then

we must ask serious questions about the relevance and importance of the incredible number of meetings we seem to generate. 'But what would we do without them?' someone asked when this issue was raised recently. 'If I didn't see other church members in meetings, I wouldn't see them at all.' Sadly, this would probably be true for many church-going Christians, which accounts for: (a) our desperate grasp on meetings as such; and (b) our very tenuous hold on any church congregation in particular. For many of us, our hold upon 'church' is in respect of certain meetings which (for the moment) we are more or less happy with, rather than in respect of people, whose importance to us is derived from the meetings, which is the only time we see them. Instead of our meetings together flowing out of the life of our relationship with one another, our relationships (such as they are) are dependent upon our attendance at meetings. Unsurprisingly, therefore, when our attendance at, or happiness with, those meetings becomes in any way problematic – for good reasons or bad – then the relationships that depend upon them become extremely fragile.

Doesn't all this illustrate just how far we are from the sort of vibrant, organic life which needs to be at the heart of the church if we are to be really attractive to those who are not yet Christians? At a time when an increasing number of unchurched people have little time or interest in what they see as 'formalised' religion, and in an age when there is a serious mistrust of organised and hierarchical institutions, we do not have merely a challenge of communication on our hands but a crisis of calling.

Simply trying to fit people into our already prepared mould of meetings is hardly going to engender a positive sense of involvement and ownership in church.

Our approach to leadership often does little to ease the problem. Institutionalised churches tend to assume that they 'need' full-time, professionally trained and qualified leaders in order to operate at all. To function without them is unthinkable, unworkable and impossible. Now, it may be true that it is entirely right and appropriate for a given church to have one or more full-time leaders or workers, but that this is a prerequisite for functioning as a church at all is, to say the least, open to question.

To allow a dependence on those who work 'full time' within the church can rob the body of believers of the opportunity of living out its calling properly. Nothing is further from the teaching of Scripture than to create a reliance on professional Christians to be the crack troops in the battle, absolving the rest of us from our responsibilities. Far from being such, full-time leaders can easily find themselves immersed in a world of pastoral responsibilities and an almost endless schedule of conferences to attend, divorced from the world inhabited by ordinary church members. Full-time pastors often admit to having so few options available to them if they were to 'come out of ministry' (as it is sometimes quaintly put) as to be virtually unemployable after a few years . . . which hardly seems the best of reasons to continue in their particular role.

Much of the energy of many full-time leaders is taken up with preparing for and servicing the weekly schedule of meetings to fulfil the expectations of the congregation who pay their wages. And the congregation themselves are able to sleep more soundly with consciences appeased by the thought that they have helped to employ someone who is able to see to it that the kingdom is advanced. What a travesty of what we are really called to be! And how important it is for those who lead to be earthed in the ordinary world from which it is so easy to become detached. One church leader recently told us how much he valued the ten hours a week he still worked in the public service sector, keeping him in touch with the everyday world outside the church. (He also added that it helped to keep him sane!)

What has emerged alongside the institutionalised church is a whole range of 'support' services which help to continue the very structures which brought them into existence in the first place. The prolific growth in the range of conferences alone is evidence of this – an expression of the service industry that has developed to help lubricate the machine we are endeavouring to keep running. It is entirely feasible to spend considerable time at conferences, fraternals, renewal days and seminars and yet fail to get to grips with the real issue of seeing our world transformed.

Many of us – and leaders especially – are working very hard: of that there is no doubt. But much, or most, of our energy is expended on keeping running the ecclesiastical machines we have set up, or which our forebears have bequeathed to us. Feeding the sausage machine; entertaining the saints; keeping the engine running; each of us can choose our own preferred metaphor. But while our best efforts are channelled into running meetings of the kind that we like, and fighting those who want to run them differently – or run them instead of us! – real evangelism and real discipleship elude us and recede like the ocean horizon.

6
The Preaching of the Gospel?

He deserves to be preached to death by wild curates. (Sydney
Smith, 1771–1845)

'Preaching,' as the venerable Martyn Lloyd-Jones put it,
'is logic on fire.' It is 'the highest and the greatest and the
most glorious calling to which anyone can ever be
called'.[1] He certainly had a long and noble history behind
him in making such claims for his own profession. Until
the rise of charismatic worship opened alternative channels for real prominence in a congregation, the struggles
within most churches had been essentially battles for
control of the pulpit. Preaching has been seen as not
merely an exposition of the word of God, but itself a sort
of secondary 'word of God'. At least, that is the strong
implication of much of the rhetoric used about it.[2]

---

[1] M. Lloyd-Jones, *Preaching and Preachers* (Hodder & Stoughton,
1971), pp 9 & 97.
[2] See, for example, the title of a recent book by P. Adam, *Speaking
God's Words: a Practical Theology of Preaching* (IVP, 1996).

The centrality of preaching is seen as part-and-parcel of the centrality of Scripture. For evangelicals, Scripture has been central, in intention at least, to their beliefs and practices. It has been this biblicism that has marked them off from Catholics who have ascribed too much author-ity to the institutional church or to tradition, and from liberals, who have assigned too much authority to human reason. (And the authority of Scripture, let us hasten to add, is an emphasis from which the present authors do not dissent.)

The suspicion of Pentecostals earlier in the twentieth century, or of charismatics by non-charismatics more recently, has been the result of fears that 'the word' was being pushed from its place at the centre of Christian life (by which was meant, of course, at the centre of Christian meetings). Even some charismatics have worried about the excesses of their more experiential brothers and sisters. And the corrective that has invari-ably been offered has been that of 'the word'. The rela-tive lack of substance in Pentecostal preaching, and the appalling ignorance of Scripture by many charismatics, have been taken as evidence that Scripture is indeed being sidelined. In each case, the remedy urged upon them has been 'the word'. However, what has generally been in mind is a particular emphasis upon the word preached (and often a particular kind of preaching at that).

Preaching is, in fact, part of our overall culture of meetings. Much is expected from it. Peculiar converting power is attributed to it and expected from it. Preaching dominates meetings as meetings dominate Christian life. Almost all of the great Christians of the past or present that most of us could easily name have been preachers. Billy Graham, Spurgeon, Wesley . . . the names trip off our tongues. Most of the leaders who are prominent among us now are prominent on the basis of their preaching. Many of us will attend special meetings, attend a conference or visit some well-known church particularly to hear a famous preacher. Preaching is openly described by many of its leading practitioners as an art-form, or theatre.[3] In most churches, a service is not considered 'organised' unless a speaker has been specified. Many church notices will give only the most basic information about the following Sunday's meetings, but will usually supply the name of the preacher. Within the evangelical tradition, 'the preaching of the word' has been credited with almost sacramental powers of much the same kind that high-church people attribute to the communion elements. As Martyn Lloyd-Jones put it, preaching is 'the primary task of the Church . . . everything else is subsidiary to this'.[4]

In the light of sentiments such as these, it is hardly surprising that some streams within evangelicalism have described it as 'the means of grace'. The importance of preaching is a major constituent element in what we have called 'the meeting syndrome'; faith comes by hearing the word of God, but this means a formal sermon, and this requires a certain kind of large, structured meeting

---

[3] See, eg, C. Morris, *Raising the Dead: the Art of the Preacher as Public Performer* (HarperCollins, 1996).

[4] M. Lloyd-Jones, *Preaching and Preachers* (Hodder & Stoughton, 1971), p 26.

... which in turn requires a certain institutionality about 'being church'.

Origins of modern evangelical preaching

Preaching is certainly in the lifeblood of evangelicalism, and has been since the beginning. By the beginning, however, we do not mean the early church but the origins of the modern evangelical movement. The early church did not have frequent, systematic or expository preaching of the kind that finds such favour in most modern congregations. This point has been argued in detail by David Norrington in his recent little masterpiece, *To Preach or Not to Preach?*, and we do not propose to repeat his arguments at (too much) length here. Norrington shows that 'preaching' in the New Testament and early church context was a much more generalised term than we might expect: preaching the gospel, for example, could refer to personal witnessing. What seems certain is that meetings did not focus Sunday by Sunday on regular preaching of the kind that dominates our services. To be sure, the practice did develop later, but only with the emergence of formalised meetings and their domination by a few designated individuals.[5]

The great evangelical preaching tradition of today has two sources: the Puritan movement of the sixteenth and seventeenth centuries and the Great Evangelical Awakening of the eighteenth. The first of these move-

---

[5] D.C. Norrington, *To Preach or Not to Preach?* (Paternoster, 1996), chs 1–3.

ments arose in England from the 1560s onwards, during the early part of the reign of Elizabeth I. The Puritans were attempting to protestantise the country as firmly and as fast as possible, and to 'purify' (hence their name) the Church of England from 'the rags of popery', a phrase which referred to clerical robes and vestments, which they detested, but the principle applied to any other aspect of religious or national life which they thought smacked of the Roman Catholic past. In this climate, a massive public education campaign seemed to be called for. This was particularly so because most pre-Reformation clergymen had been uneducated. As a result, many people, especially the illiterate peasantry, had little idea of the basics of Christianity, whether Catholic or Protestant; their religion was mostly an amalgam of quasi-Christian superstitions. Puritan preaching was designed to remedy this situation by making a strong, systematic, didactic element the centre of all church services. It also served to stress that Protestantism was a religion of the book – the Bible – and not of semi-magical sacraments.

The type of preaching adopted was borrowed from the Puritans' Reformed heroes on the continent: Calvin, Bullinger, Beza and others, but especially the first of these. These men considered systematic exposition of biblical passages to be their ideal. This pattern was not taken from Scripture itself (there is no evidence that Jesus preached his way phrase by phrase through Jeremiah to his disciples, for example, or that Peter or Paul or John did anything of the sort). The habit was borrowed from the style of scholarship of the

Renaissance, the great artistic and intellectual movement which, starting in Italy, reshaped ideas across Europe about learning, painting, science and theology during the century before the Reformation. The ideal Renaissance scholar was one who, to show his learning, provided a sentence-by-sentence commentary on a writing from classical antiquity, tying up particular turns of phrase in its original language with similar usages in other works, or commenting on the rhetorical devices employed.

Calvin himself is a prime case in point. Before his conversion, he had made his name with a commentary on a book, the *De Clementia* by the pagan writer of ancient Rome, Seneca. When he was converted and turned to preaching, Calvin gave Scripture the same treatment; it was the scholarly thing to do! Most of the other Reformers did the same. As a consequence, the tradition of Reformed preaching remains today a highly structured, methodical, logical and rhetorical discourse. It tends to require a fair degree of scholarship – or at least the appearance of such – by the preacher. (Think of those sometimes unnecessary allusions to 'the original Greek' in sermons you have heard!)

The Reformed ideal of a pastor was the scholar-preacher, who had Scripture and the Church Fathers at his fingers' ends. In more recent years, knowledge of the Church Fathers has been less a prerequisite than knowledge of the writings of the Puritans themselves. The ideal pastor's study has rows of orderly shelves, with neat series, or sets, of books on them. Note: the books should not be open on the desktop, but pristine on the shelves;

THE PREACHING OF THE GOSPEL?

the ideal impression is not of an ongoing and active
engagement with other minds, but of a meticulously cat-
alogued and mastered possession of them, to be trotted
out when occasion demands. The orderly sets of match-
ing spines are evidence that the work has been com-
pleted, not that it is in continuous flow. If the visitor to
the study is suitably overawed by this spectacle, then
actual production of evidence that the preacher does in
fact know his sources will hopefully not be required too
often! Cynicism or satire aside, our point is that this
model of preaching is a vision of patriarchy. The priestly
interpreter of Catholicism has been replaced by an all-
wise scholar-interpreter.

The second element in the evangelical preaching tradition is very different from the first, but in recent practice,
at least, has proved entirely compatible with it, though
both types continue to exist in isolation in some cases.
This second source is located in the Great Evangelical
Awakening of the eighteenth century, and is what we
might call (being vivid at the risk of being overly sarcas-
tic) the 'rabid prophet' model. Outbursts of emotion
and strong exhortation were the strength of early
Methodism, and of the movements that flowed from it.[6]
The Awakening itself was influenced by Pietism, which

---

[6] The historian David Bebbington, like most of his peers, locates the
birth of 'evangelicalism' (in anything like the modern meaning of that
term) in these eighteenth-century developments. He designates the
distinctive characteristics as: crucicentrism, conversionism, biblicism
and activism. See D. Bebbington, *Evangelicalism in Modern Britain*
(Unwin Hyman, 1989), pp 2–3.

laid less stress on doctrine and more on personal spiritual experience, and the experiential element became stronger with the passing of time. The emotionalism became more raw, especially in the revivalism that became such a constant feature of religious life on the American frontier.

It is this style that was being referred to by the American president Abraham Lincoln when he said, 'When I hear a man preach, I like to see him act as if he were fighting bees.' The tendency of preachers to shout and declaim, to crack jokes and tell weepy stories, comes from this tradition, not from the Puritans. It has little time for doctrine, but lays much stress on getting the hearer to make an emotional response. It became strongly embedded in Methodistic and, later, Pentecostal styles of preaching, and has spread in more recent years to many charismatic churches of different types. The heightened emotional state of the preacher – especially as evidenced by shouting – is generally held to imply a particular anointing by the Holy Spirit. Much evidence is therefore laid on the *informal*, or 'spiritual', authority of the preacher to propel his (or, very occasionally, her) hearers into making whatever kind of a response the sermon is indicating.

In the first model, then, the preacher is following in the tradition of the Puritans, of which he may well be acutely conscious, who in turn derived their method from the Renaissance, of which fact he is probably unaware. In the second model, he is following the stream of evangelicalism which flows from the early Methodists, via the Salvation Army and the Holiness movement, down to modern Pentecostalism and the various charismatic groupings.

In practice, as all readers will be aware, both of these models are nowadays combined by most preachers. With some, especially Reformed ministers or those who have had theological training, the first model is more in evidence, while in others it is the second. But few have any hesitation about – or even consciousness of – borrowing freely from the 'other' model where it suits their purpose.

The really significant thing is that *both* models cast the preacher in the role of hero. In the first case he is the all-wise patriarch educating his congregation who, if they are truly acting out their own designated parts, should be taking notes with their Bibles open. In the second case he is a prophet of the Lord delivering himself of an intolerable burden. We should hardly be surprised that the centrality of preaching amounts to the centrality of preachers. And no amount of disclaimers – most of them no doubt completely sincere – that the preacher is 'not preaching himself, but Christ crucified' can evade this very obvious point. Clearly, all of the really good men and women who preach in our pulpits Sunday by Sunday should be – and presumably are – out to promote, not themselves, but their understanding of the Scriptures, or a message from God. At least, we hope that this is so. We have both been preachers ourselves for many years and, unless all of our friends and relatives are disgusting syco-phants – and we have bruises to prove the contrary – we are apparently quite good at it. Most of the time, anyway. Neither do we intend to abandon preaching now. We are not attacking preaching as such, nor the Renaissance methodology, nor the expository sermon. We are merely calling attention to the effects of an overemphasis on preaching upon our total church culture, and in particular its deep complicity in creating 'the meeting syndrome'.

Preaching in a postmodern culture

Preaching can be helpful – even necessary – within certain contexts. Those contexts, however, are much more circumscribed than the evangelical tradition has generally been willing to accept. A sermon can do good where it is a form of currently necessary exhortation, applicable to all – or almost all – local Christians, regardless of their circumstances or how long they have been in the faith. An example might be a call to steadfastness on the outbreak of persecution, or guidance on how to respond to some local or national development likely to make life difficult for all Christians. The classic evangelistic sermon to non-Christians, though less and less productive in our own culture, is an obvious example of where a sermon can, under the right conditions, be very productive (although, as we shall argue in the following chapter, these conditions are not generally met with in contemporary Britain, though they are in parts of the United States). Again, a sermon might be called for to reflect on the success or otherwise of a major project in which an entire local congregation has been involved. Christians, too, need 'reminding' of the gospel, its content, its implications and its centrality, and there will be times when this end is most effectively achieved via preaching.

There might be many such possibilities for the creative and useful delivery of sermons. But they are best kept to what they were in the early church, occasional (in both senses of that word) discourses. Even then, we could learn from Jesus' style of teaching by 'telling stories and leaving people with personal space to decide for themselves how to respond to his message', or even from that of Paul, whose late-night teaching session at Troas was most likely two-way (the term used is the root of our word 'dialogue'), rather than a lengthy monologue.[7]

The real objections to the centrality of sermons are fourfold. Firstly, they tend to emphasise the centrality of preachers, with all of the unhealthy effects upon relationships that that implies. In the second place, the centrality of sermon-preaching demands a way of 'being church' more conducive to a public institution model than the family model. Thirdly, sermons have a tendency to disempower their hearers. Fourthly, they are manifestly a failure as a means of teaching and instructing Christians.

To deal with the first point, it is impossible to ignore the primary message put across in every sermon, before the preacher has even opened his or her mouth:

By using the regular sermon the preacher proclaims each week, not in words, but in the clearest manner possible, that, be the congregation never so gifted, there is present, for that period, one who is more gifted and all must attend in silence upon him (less often her).[8]

---

[7] J. Drane, *Evangelism for a New Age* (Harper, 1994), p 137.

[8] D. Norrington, *To Preach or Not to Preach?*, p 75.

Of course, defenders of the great art of preaching will say that the spiritual authority of the preacher *qua* preacher and their personal authority as individuals are two different things; that one must not reject every practice on mindlessly egalitarian grounds simply because it gives one person more prominence than another; that only charlatans really preach to gain power over others. And so on.

These are substantial arguments, but this is not the place to take issue with them. In point of fact, we believe that the distinction between private *persona* and public office is easier to maintain in respect of relatively anonymous institutions such as law courts and council officials than in the (supposed) intimacy of a congregational fellowship, and that either the distinction is bound to grow weaker or the church will approximate to the formality of the public institution. We are also inclined to think that there is no clear-cut category of 'charlatan' or wicked manipulator, and that a mixture of motives lurks within every person, every Christian and every preacher.[9] The effects of such regular dominance over a group of people as preaching bestows upon the person who is given such powers of domination are not likely to

---

[9] One excellent pastor known to us advised fellow preachers at a conference: 'Never let the congregation relax . . . you've got to create a measure of insecurity in your listeners.' This advice, given in a context which made it plain that he had the best spiritual interests of ordinary congregations at heart, illustrates well the fine line (non-existent line, some might say) between this approach to 'ministry' and manipulation. It certainly is not an approach calculated to empower hearers!

make for humility or encourage the other good qualities within the murk of our inner lives. But we do not insist upon these arguments, for the objections of the defenders of preaching really do have a lot of validity.

Our point is that the centrality of preaching simply is not saleable in a culture which tends to deconstruct every human relationship to its power constituents. Preaching so obviously functions as 'power over' those being preached to (certainly if it is the regular staple of 'being church') that it is virtually impossible, even for Christians, to understand the relationship so created in any other way. When we take account of the fact that many preachers (no worse and no better than many worship leaders, youth leaders, housegroup leaders and others of prominence in our churches) do in fact use their 'ministries' to bolster their own standing, then the argument that preaching need not necessarily be so used, deployed in an age that is so suspicious of all power relationships and addicted to (admittedly often mindless) egalitarianism, will convince fewer and fewer people. It will, in fact, become an obstacle to the gospel. Of course, this would be no persuasive objection at all if the institution of regular public preaching were a part of that very gospel, or even a subsidiary biblical injunction.[10] But in fact it is no such thing. It is, as we have described, a piece of cultural baggage that we have picked up along the way. And none the worse (or better) for that.

---

[10] For example, we do not soften the scriptural line concerning sexual morality, or the reality of divine judgement, simply because these are unpopular ideas.

The weight attached to dislike of the preacher, or of the preaching, by so many church-leavers and church-switchers is also good evidence that the power-effect of preaching repels Christians too. Christians feel threatened – or angered, or irritated – by a particular preacher in a way that makes them antagonistic towards an entire church. And this becomes a decisive factor in leaving a congregation more frequently than any other aspect of church life except relationship breakdown and worship styles. Although most of those leaving a church because of its preaching would wish to insist that they are objecting only to a particular preacher or a particular style, the issue matters to them as much as it does because, consciously or subconsciously, they recognise the power-implications of preaching: if the preaching is like *that* (whatever it is that bothers them), then to remain means to submit to its demands, or to assent to its values.

In respect of the second point, the dynamics of making preaching the centre of a meeting militate decisively against church-as-family and in favour of church-as-public-institution. Although feedback to a sermon is theoretically possible, it needs to be contrived and is, in practice, quite rare. Few shy souls would contribute encouragement – far less criticism – in what is clearly a public meeting. The very geography of meeting-places conducive to 'giving a sermon' is, by the same token, unconducive to every-member participation. A pulpit needs to be prominent – probably amplified – so that everyone can hear. Other seating needs to be made orderly and facing, not one another, but the preacher. And that is the case even in the rented school hall. In eighteenth- and nineteenth-century chapels and parish churches the formality brought about by the centrality of preaching is manifest in the very architecture, whose silent message is that 'people are there to sit and listen, and in many churches it is physically impossible to do anything else'.[11]

Concerning our third point – the tendency of sermons to disempower their hearers – preaching squeezes out space for other gifts in Christian meetings. A congregation might contain 100 people, a considerable proportion of whom may have insights, prophecies, prayers or just plain news to offer. But the sermon has the effect of crowding out these gifts, and the people who could bring them. The style of meeting which the sermon demands will deter the shy in any case, but even where some space *is* made, a huge disparity in time and importance separates the hurried, token contribution of a minute or two from the 'proper' or 'main' contribution which is, of course, the sermon. It is a case of either/or: *either* one is a contributor of a quick piece of ephemera *or* one is the nominated preacher, whose name has been given out in the notices of the previous week. The difference in status between the individual contribution and the sermon is never in doubt.

In a spectator-oriented society, preaching also encourages passivity and dependence on the preacher. This is fairly easily seen in the adulation accorded to various speakers by their respective 'fan clubs'. This may exist at a local level within a congregation, or at a

---

[11] J. Drane, *Evangelism for a New Age*, p 135.

national or even international level. Many Christians will travel a long way to hear X because they enjoy his preaching, without any necessary correlation between that enjoyment and a transformation of the hearers' lives. Any readers who doubt this need only refer themselves to their own responses to recent sermons. If we go to hear a sermon on, say, prayer, none of us will come away talking to one another about prayer; we will be talking about whether or not it was a good sermon. Yet it is of no significance at all whether or not the sermon was good; all that matters is that we deepen our prayer lives (or whatever it was that the sermon was about). By the middle of the week, most of us cannot even remember with any clarity what the sermon was about; far less will we have internalised its message. This feature of church life is ubiquitous, and in itself almost conclusive proof of the near-uselessness of preaching as it is mostly practised within the Christian subculture. The sermon itself is largely de-skilling of its hearers, unless we are very careful indeed, and contributes to 'the creation of a dependent, unreflective, semi-literate, relatively skill-less population, almost devoid of creativity'. Ironically, as Norrington remarks, the good sermon and the good preacher can be even more harmful in this respect than the bad, because they put their hearers in greater awe of the skills employed, create greater dependency and do more to inhibit real action (unless one counts coming to the front at the end of the sermon) by their hearers![12]

---

[12] D.C. Norrington, *To Preach or Not to Preach?*, pp 75–6, 78.

Finally, there is 'the obvious fact', to which John Drane calls attention, 'that much of what we think is "teaching" is not getting through anyway'.[13] Sermons are manifestly not succeeding, in contemporary cultural conditions at least, in teaching Christians about their faith. It is at least debatable whether they ever did, though that is not an argument we need to enter into here. What is beyond dispute is that the biblical knowledge – to say nothing of an ability to think Christianly about their own lives – of most Christians is little short of abysmal. Many who have been Christians for a number of years do not know one end of their Bible from the other. In sharp contrast with the early church, many candidates for baptism are unable to give a coherent account of even the most basic elements of the Christian faith ('I know that Jesus has died for my sins' or some such), and instead fall back on 'testimonies' of how they were drawn into the fellowship of the church, or 'came to feel' they should be baptised. An exercise one of us undertook with a group of long-time Christians required them to jot down, in three jargon-free sentences, the basics of the gospel as they would explain it to an unbeliever: most really struggled. If sermons informed us and educated us, this picture would be quite different.

Of course, it is possible – even likely – that sermons would equip us better if they began to emphasise the indicative a little more and the imperative a little less. In other words, there is a crying need to increase instruction and teaching, especially about the basic doctrinal and

---

[13] J. Drane, *Evangelism for a New Age*, p 135.

ethical requirements of Christian faith. There is a corresponding need to move away from the emotional arm-twisting type of sermon designed to end in an appeal or a 'time of ministry' – however much some members feel they 'need' it as a weekly cathartic 'fix', and despite so many of its apparent but sometimes illusory gains. As with so many things, it is not a case of banishing exhortation entirely in favour of exposition, but of redressing a balance.

The fact remains, however, that we inhabit a culture in which learning from spoken words is very difficult. Countless studies demonstrate that most people remember only a tiny fraction of what they have heard; most of us are increasingly visually oriented. TV is the dominant medium of our society. We may deplore this (and one of the authors has chosen not to possess a TV), but we are unlikely to communicate effectively to people who have been brought up on the flickering box, and whose leisure time is still dominated by it, without taking this factor into account. Most importantly, attention spans are getting shorter – fifteen to twenty minutes is likely to be a maximum, not just for young people, but for many adults. In the light of this, most preachers have gone for 'dumbing down' and entertainment value in order to hold the attention of their audiences at all. The result, enhanced by the tendency of most people to read less of anything including their Bibles than they did a generation ago, has been to leave most Christians overawed by their preachers but not instructed. (If they are not overawed, of course, they are likely to be disaffected.)

The difficulty of feedback and discussion in the context of large meetings means that very few really engage with the material that is being discussed. Perhaps even more importantly, the centrality of preaching in an increasingly post-literate, visually oriented society helps to make 'church' an impenetrable subculture for the unchurched. The irony is, of course, that this impenetrability is being generated at the very point – the large meeting – which we have turned into our 'shop front'.

* * *

Despite all of the more negative points that we have made here, we want to affirm that preaching is an important activity which has much to contribute to the life of a healthy church. For readers – especially preachers – who have been outraged by this chapter, that will seem an odd statement, but the *caveats*, disclaimers, qualifications and saving clauses are there for those who want to glance back over the preceding pages and look for them. Our quarrel is not with preaching as such as much as with its over-regularity and centrality in church life, which has been a major contributor to the cult of 'the meeting'. It is the centre of most of those meetings, and the generator – as well as the subject – of much of the hype that surrounds them.

Theoretically a vehicle for instruction, sermons actually leave most of us uninformed about our faith. Either we are overawed by the abilities of the speaker and thus left with a tendency to despise our own, different gifts as if they were somehow inferior, or else we are repelled or offended by the style or content of the preaching, and as a result inclined to leave the fellowship. The centrality of preaching casts the destiny of each church on the abilities of perhaps just one person; in countless cases over the past few decades, the rise and decline of a congregation has hinged almost entirely on the ability of its main preacher to draw a crowd. All readers of this book will be able to recall discussions they have had about the fortunes of their own, or some neighbouring church, over a period of time. If it has grown, it has been because so-and-so has taken over as minister and can conduct a good meeting (especially preach a good sermon). If it has declined (splits aside), it is because a good preacher has left or retired and the new one is not as good. This, we suggest, is a ridiculous state of affairs and no good witness to the gospel. The centrality of preaching means the centrality of preachers, and turns the fellowship of Christian family into a public institution.

Finally, the heavy stress upon personal authority, which is so clearly implicit in preaching, and upon listening to the propounding of abstractions for forty or fifty minutes at a time are not culturally sensitive in a postmodern age. We propose that a profound rethink is in order concerning the form, the content, the manner of delivery and the frequency of sermons. Most of all, they need freeing from their present heavy implication in 'the meeting syndrome' which renders us so powerless to act – or even to be fully 'Christians' – outside of a late-night, sweaty 'gathering of God's people'.

7

Whence Revival?

If the centrality of preaching in the life of the church is a mistaken emphasis, what does this imply for our view of revival? Revival is a major concern for evangelicals of all kinds. We all long to see thousands – indeed, millions – of people come to repentance and faith in Christ. The more we look at the ungodliness and unhappiness of the world around us, the more we are convinced that the two are linked. And even if they were not, any happiness outside of Christ is a fool's paradise in the light of what we know from the biblical revelation about God's judgement on sin. The need of the hour – of any hour – is surely for revival. We have been calling for it for a long time. Since Leonard Ravenhill's classic *Why Revival Tarries* and Arthur Wallis's *In the Day of Thy Power – the Scriptural Principles of Revival* in the 1950s, evangelicals have been analysing what they are doing wrong (or failing to do right) that is standing in the way of revival.

Prayer has been highlighted as a necessity, as has the need for holy living and a 'burden for souls'. Some groups have indicated that God would bless the church if only all Christians would move over to an uncritically pro-Israel political stance. Some new church movements have written and taught that revival would follow naturally from the restoration of what they took to be a biblical church order. A few years ago one visiting American preacher famously (or notoriously) prophesied the outbreak of revival in Britain within months. When this failed to happen, the prophecy was at first reinterpreted as meaning that revival would only 'begin to happen' at the date indicated, but this could only work as a stalling measure, and within a year he was forced to concede that a mistake had been made.

The Toronto Blessing was claimed as being a revival. After all, does not judgement begin with the household of faith? Didn't the children of Israel need to 'return unto the Lord' on occasions during the Old Testament? But such spiritualising aside, what everyone understands by 'revival' is a large-scale turning to Christ by unbelievers, and when this failed to happen on any significant scale, the 'Blessing' too was reinterpreted as being simply a 'time of refreshing'.

By 1996, attention was increasingly focused upon Pensacola in Florida, where an undoubted revival really had broken out. The number of conversions was very considerable, and any amount of latitude over the interpretation of the figures could not hide the fact that this was the real thing! Back in Britain, one prominent Anglican charismatic prophesied that revival would show up here on Pentecost Sunday, 1997, the Holy Spirit apparently undertaking to fit in neatly with his allotted slot in the liturgical calendar. The day has come and gone, however, and we're still waiting. Why?

The cartoon in our heads

The authors do not presume to have the key to revival in their pockets. But we can point to a demonstrably false assumption that we have all been making about revival which, if our analysis is anywhere near the mark, is causing our efforts to be self-defeating and is pushing revival further away.

First of all, it's worth asking what we mean by 'revival'.[1] It's one of the few definitions of a historical term in which our popular mind's-eye picture does not let us down. It conjures up images of hundreds – perhaps thousands – of people in worship meetings singing, crying, repenting, some coming to the point of conversion. Perhaps we imagine it taking place in an old Welsh chapel, or perhaps out of doors; it does not matter, for both are correct. And over the entire proceedings, of course, stands the towering figure of the preacher who, with a voice like thunder, is warning his hearers of the

---

[1] There is, admittedly, a tendency by some to broaden the term to include any period of the Christian past of which they personally approve. Thus the Reformation has been referred to as 'revival', as have the Lollard and Hussite movements. D.W. Bercot, *Will the Real Heretics Please Stand Up?* (Scroll Publishing, 1989), p 149, even considers the high-church Oxford movement as 'a revival movement' on no firmer basis than his personal approval of it. But this is so much rhetoric, however; what the term 'revival' has meant historically is the rapid growth of the church by large-scale conversions.

need to flee the wrath to come. Our imaginations can hardly let us down in this area because revival is, to such a large degree, a product of the historical imagination. Lest that seem an outrageous statement, it should swiftly be added that the revivals really did happen! Indeed, as we can see in Pensacola, they still do. The work of our imaginations is simply our (not very intelligent) insistence that *only* the kind of events that match this description qualify as 'revivals' at all. The church of Jesus Christ has grown fast – even dramatically – in many parts of the world independently of frothy meetings.

Before considering cases of revival which do *not* fit our 'cartoon image', however, it is worth considering which actual historical instances do fit. Which real events might have inspired the picture in our mind's eye, in which hundreds of conversions come out of rapid conviction induced by a meeting, a sermon, or some other one-off experience? The obvious examples, of course, relate to some events in the book of Acts: Peter's sermon on the Day of Pentecost, following which 3,000 were baptised, and some, at least, of Paul's evangelism in the synagogues of Asia Minor. Then probably most of us would get stuck, and for our next example would have to 'fast forward' almost 1,700 years to Britain in the 1730s: the eighteenth-century Methodist Awakening took place under the ministries of John Wesley, George Whitefield and others (in England), and of Daniel Rowland, Hywel Harris and others (in Wales), as well as smaller scale, but also important, revivals in Ireland and Scotland.

At the same time, some of the colonies in North America witnessed dramatic scenes – one thinks of the great revivalist and theologian Jonathan Edwards. Wales saw a succession of local revivals in the nineteenth century, as well as a larger, national one in 1859 which saw about 110,000 people coming to faith. Ireland also saw revival during the same year. America witnessed a host of local revivals, especially on 'the frontier' as it moved westwards with the wagon trains. The great preacher Charles Grandison Finney introduced a whole host of 'New Measures' – altar calls, praying for people by name, 'anxious seats' – and other devices which became the stocks-in-trade of later evangelists.

And what of the twentieth century? One thinks, of course, of the Welsh revival of 1904–5, which saw about 100,000 conversions, and of the much smaller Hebridean awakening of the 1950s, the most recent on British soil. But these last two are perhaps hardly the summit at which we should be aiming; they took place against the background of the long-term decline of evangelicalism in Britain, which lasted down to well after the mid-century, and did nothing to arrest it. Nowadays, the 'frothy-meeting' kind of revival is most likely to happen in sub-Saharan Africa (think of Reinhard Bonnke) or South America.

Two kinds of revival

And what do all of these examples have in common? All of them, without exception, were, or are, cultures in which the basics of the gospel were known by a large swathe of the population before the heroic preacher ever opened his mouth. The Jews on the Day of Pentecost knew who God was, what the moral law was, what sin was, and that they had committed it. Indeed, they even knew who Jesus was, for he had been walking among them a few weeks before! All they needed was the good news of a Saviour. The countries of Britain in the eighteenth century all had this awareness to an even greater degree. Most of the population had been specifically Protestant for several generations. Protestantism-and-water though much of popular religiosity may have been, it was nevertheless enough to provide the background knowledge necessary for people to come under conviction of their sins, and to be readily persuadable that Jesus was a Saviour.[2]

The historian Michael Watts shows that an analysis of

---

[2] The point is often made that the state of religion in the countries of Britain before the Awakening was at a deplorably low ebb. Our rejoinder is twofold. In the first place, preachers' rhetoric has almost always been employed in decrying the particular evils of their age in terms of a decline from what had existed before. (Our own age is a case in point.) This is not to discount all such claims, but it does mean that they cannot simply be taken at face value. In the case of the early eighteenth century, they are particularly suspect. Enthusiastic historians of Methodism have tended to exaggerate the (admittedly bad) state of affairs prior to the Awakening, in order to magnify the significance of the Methodist achievement. For argument, see G.H. Jenkins, *Protestant Dissenters in Wales 1639–1689* (University of Wales Press, 1992) pp 2–4; G.H. Jenkins, *Literature, Religion and Society in Wales 1660–1730* (University of Wales Press, 1978), pp 305–9. In the second place, the lack of true spirituality is irrelevant to our case; the fact remains that the worldview and most of the cognitive claims of basic Christianity were shared by the target audience of the Methodist evangelists.

converts to Methodism in the eighteenth and nineteenth centuries reveals most of them to have been reared in godly homes.[3] The dramatic meeting acted simply as the final nudge towards conversion. 'Revival' can happen now in South America because most people know at least most of the essential elements of the gospel from their Catholic cultural background. Something similar is true across much of Africa, where a basic belief in central Christian ideas is similarly entrenched, particularly as a result of the mission schools, which have inculcated both Christian ideas and the value of literacy. But it's not true in India or China, which is why we don't associate those countries with the 'revival' of our imaginations, even though the latter now has a huge number of Christians.

And it's not true either in Britain. Facing this reality comes hard to the 'hot Prots' who want to insist that this is still, in some Heath-Robinsonian sense, a 'Christian country'. But it isn't, and no amount of spiritual rhetoric can make it true. The fact is that most people – certainly most people under fifty – have no idea at all what the Christian faith is about. Certainly there is no clear conception of what the word 'God' means, or moral absolutes, or even moral obligations; most Westerners think instead in terms of rights, which has the important consequence of making them unable to see themselves as sinners and so in need of salvation.

Our missionary situation is much more similar to that of Paul in Athens who was told, at the end of his first

---

[3] M. Watts, *The Dissenters* (OUP, 1978, 1995), vol 1, pp 421–8; vol 2, pp 160–4.

evangelistic effort, 'We will hear you again concerning this' (Acts 17:32). The same was true with other outreaches to Gentiles who had never been anywhere near a synagogue. These total pagans had no such knowledge as the Jews or the 'God-fearers' had. Since pagans of this sort were the vast bulk of the target audience for Christian evangelism in the second and third centuries, Christian methods of evangelism switched sharply to a gradualist approach. The church continued to grow fast, but it did not rely on hosts of instant decisions on the back of a sermon or a meeting. The pagans needed, as our neighbours need, careful, slow explanation and example over a period of time. Our context demands hard work, not hysteria. We can have a revival on something closer to this model (which is similar in some ways to the current revival in China), but not of the kind that fits the stereotype in our heads.

To those who will point to Pensacola, the reply is obvious. These places are part of the 'Bible belt', and always have been. When such things happen in New England or Quebec, then the hypothesis we've been outlining here will be proven to be wrong. But not before. Our missionary situation is that of Acts 19, not that of Acts 2.

Revival can certainly happen here, but when it does it will not be off the back of a sensational meeting or a barnstorming sermon, because our neighbours simply aren't listening. If we're serious about revival, shrieking at the tops of our voices may pay dividends in Tanzania or Tennessee, but in Tooting Bec and Tyneside we'll do better running an Alpha course.

So what holds us back?

The trouble is, most of us are so conditioned to thinking of revival as looking like the cartoon image in our heads, that we have trouble in thinking of the results of so many Alpha groups – or one to one, gradual evangelism of any kind – as constituting revival at all. The authors' greatest fear is that this chapter will be heard as saying that revival is not possible in our present situation. But we mean just the opposite. Revival is certainly possible, but only if we stop insisting that revival must conform to the Acts 2/Great Awakening model. Obsession with that pattern while ignoring the cultural specifics of our own situation means that, yet again, we focus all of our hopes on large public meetings. And that is a futile hope, as the experience of the last few decades has shown. Of course, the idea that revival will somehow appear out of an even more sensational meeting than the one we had last week, or an even more dramatic sermon, may appeal to the push-button mentality in which we Westerners are all so thoroughly steeped, but then we must recognise that we are projecting our own values *onto* Scripture, not deriving our values *from* it.

The suddenness of conversion in Acts 2 does not make meeting-generated instant revival normative, any more than the gradualness of conversions in Acts 17–19 makes *that* pattern normative; each is the right approach for the particular evangelistic context. Neither approach is more 'spiritual' than the other – but using the appropriate model for the situation makes a lot more sense than using the wrong one.

The way things are at the moment, the burden for producing revival is placed upon a vehicle – the meeting –
that, in our culture at least, can never produce it. Non-
leaders feel themselves thereby absolved of responsibility
for evangelising their neighbours and work colleagues;
the burden is upon the meeting and those who lead it. In
particular, it falls upon the sermons and those who
preach them. Many political and religious groups have
been sneered at for falling into the trap of 'believing their
own rhetoric'; modern evangelicals must be the only
group to fall into the snare of believing their own
rhetoric *about* their own rhetoric, i.e. preaching. The
exhortations of many preachers that revival will happen
if only we do x, or perform y more faithfully, or rid ourselves of besetting sin z, do more to make a stirring
sermon, and so a stirring meeting, than they do to bring
revival nearer. They are at best discouraging, and ulti-
mately undermining of faith, because the expectation of
revival is never met. And neither can it be, the way we are
going about it.

Prayer and holiness of life are doubtless important in
seeking God for revival. (Though the church immedi-
ately prior to the Methodist Awakening was not notably
excellent in these respects.) But if reproducing the
rhetoric, manners and mores of the Puritans (especially
the value of expository preaching) was the prerequisite
for revival, then those sections of evangelicalism which
most stress these things would be experiencing revival. In
fact they are shrinking even as a share of the evangelical
constituency, and have been for a generation. If 'New
Testament church government' by apostles and prophets

brought revival, then the rise of the New Churches would have seen it happen, yet despite their impressive and laudable successes in Britain, we are not yet in a revival situation here. If the Toronto Blessing or any other type of ecstatic meeting brought revival, it would be in full swing right now. But here we are. Waiting. The authors have the temerity to suggest that we all try, with prayer and holiness, a little evangelism. Not in the meetings. Not by our leaders. But by us. At home. At work. At play. Not in expectation of instant results, but sowing, explaining, persuading, listening, answering questions.

Laurence Singlehurst, as ever bringing bucketloads of good sense to this subject, points out the need for churches to 'make space' for their members to make non-Christian friends:

> We may have to face the issue that our programme is so busy with church meetings that there is hardly any time for people to form relationships with those outside the church. We will have to make some radical decisions if we are going to create time for people to build relationships.[4]

For, as with second- and third-century pagans, that is the only way the vast bulk of our neighbours, who understand nothing of our faith and are hostile to the little they do understand, will hear us. Only this is truly 'preaching the gospel' – and 'How can they believe in the one of whom they have not heard? And how can they hear without someone preaching to them?' (Rom 10:14).

---

[4] L. Singlehurst, *Sowing, Reaping, Keeping* (Crossway, 1995), p 107.

When Paul spoke of 'preaching' he was not thinking of a hero, a crowd and a four-point sermon. He was thinking of us.

Most of us became Christians this way ourselves, if we're honest. Surveys indicate that, thirty years ago, 69 per cent of evangelicals in Britain could put a date on their conversion. Nowadays a majority of exactly the same size cannot do so, and testify to having become Christians over a period of time.[5] Research indicates that most people who become Christians need between five and seven positive experiences of Christians and Christianity.[6] What's true for us will be even more true in respect of productive evangelism going on right now and in the future. The Alpha groups again, or something yet more radical.

Most of us, however, want revival to come out of our meetings. As a result, it is meetings in which we invest our time, effort and emotional energy. And it is in meetings that we put our faith. When leaders claiming a prophetic anointing predict revival for such and such a time and such and such a place, the almost inevitable accompanying inference is that it will be a meeting-induced revival. Time and again, the promised revival fails to materialise. The faith of those involved is built up only to be dashed. (As with all meetings, those which do not reinforce faith inevitably tend to reduce it.) So this approach to revival does not merely fail to deliver; it actually pushes revival

---

[5] *Land Marc*, Spring 1993, as cited in D. Tomlinson, *The Post-Evangelical* (SPCK, 1995), p 143.

[6] L. Singlehurst, *Sowing, Reaping, Keeping*, p 26.

further away. It does this in two ways: firstly by ending up discouraging those of us who are Christians already, and secondly by getting us to invest our energies in the wrong place – in meetings.

Creating a fringe

If we put more of our time into building positive relationships with those around us, we would have a much bigger pool to fish from. In any case, historically, in virtually all circumstances and all types of revival, the majority of those who have made decisions to follow Christ were 'fringers'. In other words, they had at least some previous contact with Christians or the church. Our problem is that the fringe has vanished in recent years.

There are a number of reasons for this. One is the growing cult of privacy in Western societies. People tend, more and more, to live isolated, private lives outside of working hours; people belong to fewer clubs like Scouts or Guides, visit the cinema and the theatre less and (the recent upturn notwithstanding) attend fewer football matches than they did fifty years ago. Consequently, churches impinge less and less on the consciousness of those who are not actually their members; faith becomes more and more of a private affair. Another reason is the move away from Christian-based beliefs about morality or anything else. In consequence, those who are not actually committed Christians are unlikely to have anything to do with church, or send their children to its youth clubs or Sunday school.

This means that churches have to work harder to create such a fringe. Mother-and-toddler groups are one frequent strategy, but we need many more ideas. Workplace organisations are particularly badly needed. So too are imaginative one-off events, particularly if these are not overtly evangelistic, and allow non-Christians to attend and/or participate on equal terms. We frequently fail to appreciate the negative image of Christianity and of Christians that we have to overcome before we can establish any rapport at all with those outside. Consequently, we need to put to rest the negative images by welcoming and, above all, non-threatening contact with outsiders before there is likely to be any receptivity at all to what we have to say. Pre-evangelism needs to precede evangelism!

One really good example of this kind of activity was conducted by a church involved with a secular charity for which it wished to raise money. A music concert was organised with a wide range of talented local people asked to participate, especially teenagers. A minority of the participants, and only a small minority of those attending, were Christians. The preparations took place over a sufficiently long period of time for the majority to be reassured that they were not being 'got at' and that the event wasn't so churchy as to scare them off. There were refreshments and a couple of two-minute speeches, including one by the pastor, who promised jokily not to preach . . . and then kept his word!

No one got saved. But the effect was terrific nonetheless. Bridges had been built to many people who now knew about the church, had darkened its doors and emerged unscathed and happy about the experience. They knew that 'God is good and Christians are OK' . . . which is a lot more than most of the population knows!

Why are we telling this story? Because most of us need to learn that reaping can only come after sowing. The eighteenth-century revivals – or those going on right now in Pensacola and sub-Saharan Africa – can reap straight away because the sowing took place automatically in the lives of everyone through the influence of churches and the Christian ideas dispersed through society as a whole. With most of the pagans surrounding us in our society, however, no sowing has ever taken place. On the contrary, all kinds of rocks have been scattered over the ground by the nature of most people's upbringing (including their education) as well as by the media. Given these unavoidable facts, precious little reaping is likely until we have done the necessary sowing. 'Low-cringe' evangelism is a good idea; 'low-fringe' evangelism, however, simply doesn't work!

For most of us, however, reaping is much more attractive than laborious sowing. Laurence Singlehurst tells about a certain town which hosted a mission with a 5,000-seater tent. The churches of the area had tried to encourage their members to spend the previous year in 'sowing', that is, in creatively making friends with people. Even so, few attended the classes on friendship evangelism. When it came to holding sessions on counselling people about making decisions for Christ at the mission itself, however, the organisers were overwhelmed; everyone wanted a piece of the action! Once again, faith had been placed in one cataclysmic meeting to do what ordinary Christians had failed to do over the preceding months and years. The fruits of the mission – or lack of them – were sadly predictable.[7]

Pinning our faith in the meeting as the fount of all blessing and the epitome of church-ness is holding revival – and even ordinary evangelism – at bay. By escaping the 'meeting syndrome', we can be free to become channels of blessing and points of contact with those who do not know Christ. Revival is an important idea, but if we can avoid becoming slaves to our own misunderstandings about the past, it can be more than an idea. It can become a reality.

---

[7] *Ibid.*, p 53.

8

Beyond Institutions: Redefining 'Church'

If the previous few chapters have sketched so much that is wrong with 'the meeting syndrome' into which we have allowed ourselves to become ensnared, how do we escape from that syndrome? In particular, how do we escape the 'culture wars' and power struggles which bedevil the internal life of so many of our churches? Even more importantly, how can we prevent the constant drift of people from one congregation, and one disillusioning experience of 'church', to another (or even worse, to none at all)?

It is our contention that we need urgently to start redefining what it means to 'be church' if we are to make any significant evangelistic progress at all, or even to conserve what we have. As things stand at the moment, the institutional aspect of church makes it – and the experience of 'being a Christian' – seem primarily to consist of so many meetings and conformity to the cultural norms and shibboleths and power structures of those meetings. This has had disadvantages in the form of spiritual shallowness and disunity, the 'cult of the leader' and (the flip-side of this) dependency and perpetuated immaturity of individual Christians. We need to start downplaying the institutionality of 'church' altogether. Only in this way can we adapt the cultural form in which the gospel is presented without violating its content.

A simple illustration illuminates the issue very well. Let us imagine two very common events in the life of Christians. A group of fifty or a hundred of us meet together in a church building, or chapel, or perhaps a rented school hall, on a Sunday morning. We sing songs, someone leads us in prayer, perhaps several of us pray aloud, someone preaches a sermon, and we conclude with a hymn. This, all will say, is 'church'. And very true that is.

In the second event several Christian friends call at your house or flat for coffee. Perhaps they are from the same Sunday congregation as you, perhaps not. Perhaps they are from another part of the country, or even from a different country. It doesn't matter. They park themselves on your carpet, and you talk together of the usual mixture of secular and spiritual things, and with the usual mixture of sadness and laughter, problems and happiness. Perhaps you pray together, perhaps not. Once again, most committed Christians would agree that this, too, is 'church'.

Yet the vast majority would, we suspect, want to add some kind of qualification to the point in respect of this second event: 'It's not "church" in quite the same way'; 'it's not *really* "church"'; 'it's part of an expression of what "church" is, but it's not "church" in itself'. These are all the kind of hesitations one might expect to hear.

The more theologically minded would probably make the point that the visit to the home was an expression of the 'universal church', whereas the former was a gathering of the 'local church'. This, also, is very true, but since it is commonly held (among Protestants, at least) that the 'universal church' has no institutional existence, and since it can never meet in one place at one time, then it is generally considered to be a purely abstract entity, a somewhat hypothetical theological construct.

If all of this sounds rather high-flown, it translates into a popular attitude that only the local – and therefore, via its meetings, the institutional – church is 'real church', while the 'universal church' is simply a spiritual way of talking about the sum total of all the Christians alive in the world at the present moment. In the face of this state of affairs, we wish to ask one simple question: Why?

Local church versus universal church?

To be sure, Scripture uses the word 'church' in both senses, though it should be remembered that *ekklesia* was a common secular word before ever the Christians picked it up, and is used as such in the New Testament (see Acts 19:32, 39, 41). So any distinctions of meaning that we place upon the word remain precisely that: our distinctions. To that extent, they are eisegetical. And eisegesis, of course, is the opposite of exegesis. Exegesis is what a good preacher or Bible teacher or commentator should do: it is, literally, 'reading out of' the text, or letting the text speak for itself and explaining its meaning to make it clearer. But eisegesis is 'reading into' the text. Generally, we do this all the time, usually in defence of our traditions or in an attempt to baptise our secular opinions with the justification of scriptural support, but we don't like to admit the fact. And the distinction between 'local church' and 'universal church' is just such a piece of eisegesis.

Now, taken by itself, this eisegetical distinction is a perfectly harmless one. It's pretty useful to be able to distinguish between a usage of the word 'tea' that applies to a beverage in your cup, and a usage that refers to a substantial proportion of India's GNP. But at the end of the day we're still talking about the same stuff. The tea doesn't become something different on the way from a vast warehouse in Darjeeling to a little sachet on your kitchen table. The different use of the word is for our convenience only. If we objectify the two usages to think that we are talking about two different things, we have made a foolish mistake. And when it comes to the word 'church', we have in fact made such a mistake. We give the word an objectified existence in the local context which is somehow different in kind from the rather ethereal meaning we have in mind when we talk about 'the worldwide church'. But in both cases, local and international, we simply mean the sum total of those who are 'in Christ'.

It makes no sense to insist that only the local congregation is church. In deference to this conception, parachurch organisations are often at pains to insist that they are not churches. Again, why not? Is a workplace Christian Union not 'church'? Would claiming that it is make one of its members somehow no longer a member of Old Town Baptist when she gets home from the office? Only if we insist on objectifying the existence of 'church' in each case, rather than happily accepting that both are 'church'. For those who are still not convinced by this argument, let us ask the question again. Is a missionary organisation a church? When looking at the congregations it has founded and runs on the mission-field, all will presumably say 'Yes'. So do its missionaries collectively cease to be a church the moment their plane lands back on the tarmac in London?

Once we have really grasped the point that the church is not an institution, but a collective way of expressing the identity of those who are 'in Christ', we are in a position to revolutionise our attitudes and behaviour into something far more productive than our present malaise. The chat over coffee is just as much 'church' as the structured meeting that leaves most of us – for good reasons or poor ones – so frustrated each Sunday. That may be bad news for those for whom such meetings are a platform for their personal influence and prominence, but it's good news for the rest of us. Of course, we recognise that the moment 'church' in any form starts to define itself (eg, a cell or housegroup), it *becomes* an institution.[1] We are not arguing that this problem be circumvented by allowing church to become *only* a series of formless chats over coffee (or whatever). But we do want to urge that the issue be minimised by a drastic reduction in the institutionality of meetings that is proving such a

---

[1] We are grateful to Gina Bulica for this valuable point.

hindrance to gaining new Christians – or even keeping them – in our postmodern Western culture. This end, we believe, is best served by refusing to objectify 'church' as an institution.

So what are meetings for?

What we are suggesting is not the abandonment of meetings; clearly they serve many useful purposes. In the first place, they can be a basis for worship and teaching (though, as we have noted in earlier chapters, public meetings are certainly not without their drawbacks in this regard). Meetings are also the appropriate settings for administering communion and baptism, along with reminders of what these things signify.

These objectives are what sociologists call the 'manifest function' of such meetings, just as the 'manifest' purpose of a funeral is to bury the person who has died. But the 'latent function' may be just as important, or even more important. A dead person, for example, will be none the wiser if they are buried in a bin-bag on waste ground by strangers. But funerals act as a focus for grief by relatives and loved ones, and serve as a formal terminus and ritual moving-on point for those who participate in them. In the light of this 'latent function', a bin-bag on waste ground would be unthinkable. In the same way, church meetings have the latent functions of providing the emotional solidarity and affirmation that comes from being part of a large crowd. They can introduce Christians to others in their area, or draw the teaching of some prominent leader to their attention, act as a noticeboard (not that anyone ever pays attention to the notices, as far as we are aware!) or act as a balance to whatever imbalances may have built up in their own network of personal relationships.

Most importantly, meetings provide cohesion and opportunities for reinforcement of faith. These things are of vital importance, which is one reason why the friction experienced by most Christians in respect of meetings is so damaging, and causes so much spiritual disarray. Basically, if a meeting does not promote cohesion between a given Christian and his or her fellows, it is likely to have the opposite effect and actually foster alienation, at least in the long term. Similarly, if a meeting does not reinforce faith, it is likely to undermine it. And here we need to consider Os Guinness's point about the need for churches to be 'plausibility structures' for the gospel. As he points out, if Christians are alienated inwardly from a poorly functioning church community, then they will inevitably slide spiritually.[2] Unless we are very hard-boiled cookies – and most of us are not – the effect of habitually visiting meetings which grate with our spiritual sensibilities, or which depend overmuch for their spiritual plausibility upon leaders in whom we have no confidence, is likely to be negative. That is why one of the first requirements of a meeting is that it makes Christian faith more believable, for those attending it, than it was before. If this need is kept clearly in mind, it should helpfully steer us clear of the temptations of self-indulgence, whether by leaders wanting

---

[2] O. Guinness, *The Gravedigger File* (Hodder, 1983), p 36.

prominence or non-leaders wanting an emotional 'wallow'.

If meetings really fulfil these functions, then they are doing valuable work; they are contributing towards the real ends of church life – worship, cohesion, discipleship and reinforcement of the faith – rather than becoming ends in themselves, and thereby causes of division and friction. The full potential benefits of meetings, therefore, are obtainable precisely by not allowing them to attain the overwhelming centrality that meetings and their ethos have come to play in the lives of most Christians. We believe that a huge scaling-down, or deconstruction, of meetings is necessary, and with it the modification of the ecclesial structures which those meetings support.

Indeed, this shift is already happening. The most successful evangelistic strategy in Britain in the 1990s has been the use of Alpha groups. These are small, informal gatherings, usually in people's homes, and with plenty of opportunity for feedback. To be sure, they have some structure, but they are nevertheless closer to the coffee-and-chat-on-your-living-room-carpet than they are to a 'church service', of whatever type. Our prediction is that this trend will continue, and ought to.

The meeting: shop-front or inner sanctum?

So much have our assumptions been shaped by the centrality of public meetings to what it means to 'be church', that it really comes as something of a surprise to be confronted by the reality of the early Christians and

their life. The church in the first three centuries was oper-
ating in a largely pagan environment, much as we are. To
be sure, many of the early converts had a background in
Judaism, either as Jews themselves, or as Gentile
hangers-on of the synagogues in Asia Minor and elsewhere (the latter group were referred to as 'God-fearers').
But beyond this limited early 'target audience', the early
Christians had similar problems to us in addressing
themselves to people who had no explicit knowledge of
God and his moral law, and no clear understanding of
themselves as made in God's image. Unsurprisingly,
these people were not susceptible to being zapped into
the kingdom by a one-off message from Paul or any of
the other apostles and evangelists. A different strategy
was needed. More surprisingly, perhaps, that strategy
was not so very different from the Alpha-group
approach!

Unfortunately, we have tended to assume that the
doorway into the church is some kind of a public
meeting. In our mind's eye, we envisage a person coming
along to one of our services, and 'making a decision' in
response to something that happens or is said there.
Then, after a few months of instruction on a foundation
course or baptism class, they are baptised and 'admitted
into membership' or whatever other formalities our
congregation requires. Only then, once they are in good
standing and numbered among the 'keenies', are they
assigned to one of our housegroups.

Early-church practice was almost the reverse of this.
The evidence shows that, in the early centuries, the circle
of personal Christian friends was the evangelistic cutting

edge of the church, not its inner bastion reserved for the committed and approved. Typically, a person became a Christian by observing the Christian lifestyle of a friend or neighbour or workmate. As their interest increased, they were drawn into the circle of Christians, where they were taught and catechised on the basics of Christian life and belief. They were also 'rehabituated'; that is, they were required to lay aside pagan and sinful practices. There had to be evidence of a thoroughgoing repentance. This process usually took some time, up to about three years, though 'If any one be diligent, and has a goodwill to his business, let him be admitted: for it is not the length of time, but the course of life, that is judged.' Basic teaching and catechising took place at the level of the home group and of ordinary Christians: 'Let him that teaches, although he be one of the laity, yet, if he be skilful in the word and grave in his manners, teach; for "they shall be all taught of God".'[3] In fact, the new convert's first experience of a large gathering of the church was at baptism. (Large meetings were often practically secret in any case, because of the pressure of persecution.)[4] The formalised meeting was not the 'store-front' or public gateway into the church, but its inner sanctum. Conversely, the home group or cell was

---

[3] *Constitutions of the Holy Apostles*, xxxii. The reference to 'laity' shows that there was already by this date (third century) a formal clergy, but they did not yet monopolise teaching as they were later to come to do and, in many cases, still do.

[4] Alan Kreider, 'Worship and Evangelism in Pre-Christendom', *Vox Evangelica* (1994), pp 7–38 gives a brilliant and scholarly exposition of these points.

not the inner sanctum, but the point of contact with the world. Thus evangelism and 'being church' were functions of ordinary Christian life, not of formalised meetings.

Slowly, under force of circumstance, we are learning to reverse our priorities to something closer to this model. Current evidence shows that most people who become Christians do so over a period of time, and through the witness of friends, rather than, say, as a result of a sermon or an experience in a meeting. Real life, then, is already out of accord with the traditional expectations of our Christian subculture. The trouble is that our church life is still largely geared to those expectations, rather than to the reality. As a result, most of our efforts, in evangelism and other things, go into the 'normative' channel of God's blessing – meetings – while most of those who actually do 'commit their lives to Christ' do so accidentally, as it were, outside of those channels. As in so many observations of church life, *The Sacred Diary of Adrian Plass* hits the nail squarely on the head. As Plass tells it, he applies all of the Christian subculture's expected techniques of evangelism, with the (for him) usual hilarious results. The humour is that when Ted, the hapless target of all this evangelism, actually does become a Christian, he does so in spite of the church meeting and the street 'witnessing', not because of it.[5]

---

[5] A. Plass, *The Sacred Diary of Adrian Plass (aged 37¾)* (Marshall Pickering, 1987), pp 30–6.

Evangelism for all, by all

What if we started to encourage what is happening anyway? What if we began to adjust our expectations, so that we demand more evangelistically – and in other ways too – of home groups and small cliques of Christian friends, and less of meetings? Why hurry to bundle converts and potential converts into public meetings, as if the minister or the worship band should do the evangelism for us? Why give the impression that 'being a Christian' is all about – or mostly about – enthusiastic participation in the subculture's quirky meetings, when at least some aspects of those meetings already irritate most of us, and will almost certainly alienate the newcomers too once the shine has worn off . . . assuming they aren't repelled by them in the first place? Instead of delegating evangelism to leaders of big meetings, why not assume primary responsibility ourselves, which is biblically where it has belonged all along? We are pleased (if a little surprised) to find ourselves in agreement with John Stott on this point:

> All so-called 'missions', because they are sporadic in character and professional in leadership, can actually discourage genuine 'mission' which is the non-stop responsibility of non-professionals.[6]

All of this becomes very much easier to handle once we have grasped the vital truth that we are church all the time, not simply when we are gathered in a formalised

---

[6] J. Stott, *Our Guilty Silence* (Hodder, 1967), p 61.

meeting. The very existence of the Alpha groups pre-supposes that Christians will have friends outside the church whom they know sufficiently well to ask along to the group. That presupposition in itself demands a change in our behaviour; having friends who are not Christians stands unmasked as the prerequisite for evangelism. It always was a prerequisite, but our false expectation that conversions would somehow material-ise through meetings allowed us to hide ourselves from that (rather obvious) reality.

Unfortunately, however, most of us who have been Christians for a long time have disappeared, socially speaking, into the parallel universe that is the Christian subculture. Laurence Singlehurst describes the situation well:

> The average Christian, when he or she is first converted, knows many non-Christians. But . . . month by month, year by year, this convert gets drawn into the Christian subculture . . . by churches having too many meetings and expectations on members which restrict the amount of free time available. As time goes by, the new believer knows fewer and fewer non-Christians until reaching that wonderful point of sanctification – no non-Christian friends![7]

Perhaps we should not be so hard on ourselves; Christian values and ideas are so much at variance with those of surrounding society that, to a certain extent at least, a Christian is not always an acceptable friend. That does not alter the fact, however, that the burden lies

---

[7] L. Singlehurst, *Sowing, Reaping, Keeping* (Crossway, 1995), p 37.

squarely upon us to bridge that gap using whatever means we can.

One attempt at such bridge-building in the Alpha context is that once contacts are made and the outsiders are coming along, they are invited to a meal before any 'sessions' are held at all. In other words, they are in a non-threatening environment where they are not being preached at! As the course gets underway, Christians and non-Christians participate on an equal basis, subject only to the need to move through the requisite material. All questions are freely discussed. The unbelievers are able to observe Christians and their real behaviour, including unguarded comments, over a period of time. Their own intellectual doubts and practical hurdles in the way of commitment can be fully addressed rather than papered over or treated only in a generalised or abstract way by a sermon delivered from a platform. And finally, they are not put under pressure.

Re-envisaging church

Alpha groups are still relatively formal and structured; they are still in some sense 'meetings'. We are not too surprised, therefore, to find that even Alpha groups can run out of steam, and it seems they are beginning to do so.[8] This will be particularly true where they become more formalised over time, or are reduced to a technique. This is because the answers to our problems are *not* techniques or new structures, this kind of meeting rather

---

[8] *New Frontiers International Magazine*, Spring 1998.

than that kind of meeting, or this leader rather than that one. These are all things about which we could argue for ever. Rather, we will grow by building bridges to others through building relationships.

Alpha groups are not a miracle cure; they simply allow people to get closer to reality – and to one another – than our large meetings do. At best, they are only one possible way ahead among many. Nevertheless, they do at least approximate more to the second- and third-century evangelism model described above. Despite their varying degrees of success – and intimations of having a definite 'shelf-life' – they are clearly more successful than anything British Christians have tried in a long time. We suggest that this is at least partly because each group can develop its own internal culture and way of proceeding, talking and behaving, thereby reducing the alienation from 'church culture' experienced by people who are (hopefully) in the process of becoming Christians.

One such group in a church known to us enjoyed themselves so much that they wanted to stay together once the course was over. (This is another example of joint activity – actually doing something together – fostering cohesion.) Sadly, but unsurprisingly, the request was turned down by the vicar of the church in question. The vicar's reasoning is not hard to guess at. If you are building an institution, then loyalty must be focused on that institution – and perhaps its leaders – not upon subsets (or factions, as he might insist) within it. But like every other church, his congregation is in fact losing members to others around it over various disgruntlements with its internal culture. So, whether they stay or leave, those unnecessary battles will now be foisted upon the new Christians from the Alpha course.

But allowing the microcosmic expressions of 'church' – whether ex-Alpha groups or clusters of friends – to act as the basis for more activity, evangelism and teaching, would increase our productivity so much! It would give the opportunity for involvement by every member; indeed, it would compel it. It would also remove a major source of frustration, discouragement and disincentive – the culture and politics of the public meeting – from its centrality in church life, and therefore from being a primary cause of tension.

The recognition that the Christian Union or similar group in the school, college or workplace is also 'church', and not some optional extra, would also, we believe, enhance our awareness of the need to be a witness in the place where we spend most of our socialising, waking hours. Perhaps it is no accident that it is organisations such as these that can gain maximum co-operation from the widest range of Christians. Within the ordinary congregation, it seems almost impossible to stop believers of the same denomination and similar theology from fighting like hens over some subsidiary issue or set of issues. But within Christian groups in the workplace, co-operation can be secured from supporters of believers' baptism and Anglicans, from charismatics and non-charismatics, from predestinarians and free-willers. And if they hold formalised worship times at all, each will (mostly) put up with the foibles of the others, for each person knows that what style of worship is adopted is immaterial to the primary purpose of the organisation.

It could not be, could it, that the obvious practical purpose of such groups secures a cohesion and a tolerance that local congregations, whose meetings are largely an end in themselves, cannot?

Let there be no misunderstanding: we are not saying that issues of baptism, or of spiritual gifts, or of doctrine, are unimportant. We hold very firm views on each of these matters and (though we are neither ashamed nor proud of the fact) have 'gone into battle' for them in various contexts. We are simply pointing out here that small, practically oriented groups based on existing relationships and tied in with real-life situations (like work, or neighbours, or friends, or school) tend to be far more productive and less quarrelsome (by and large!) than groups that have little in common except their attendance at public meetings which are primarily ends in themselves, and thus the subject of endless squabbles.

The truth is that the church of Jesus Christ is far bigger than the parochial little kingdoms that we have insisted be its primary expression. Local congregations are bound to continue to play a crucial role in pastoral work, teaching, and even evangelism. But the institutionalised expressions of those congregations, namely their public meetings, need to be drastically re-thought, so that they serve the primary functions of the church, rather than becoming the primary function themselves. In particular, the de-institutionalising of our understanding of 'church' is vital if we are to face the massive cultural shift that is taking place under our feet. For it is that shift in popular culture, in favour of choice and away from sacrosanct institutions, which will do us ever-increasing harm if we insist upon keeping our present form.

Of course, Christian witness does not require us to reflect the 'spirit of the age'; in many areas we need to be a 'sign of contradiction'. At many levels, the world's freedom-to-be-fickle attitude needs to be challenged by the gospel. But we will do ourselves no service by insisting on a confusion between the gospel (that is, the things that matter in terms of belief and ethical behaviour) and the cultural forms which we give to 'church'. As Christians, we have a very bad history of absolutising the cultural forms of a past generation and insisting that church must look like this because it is somehow part-and-parcel of the gospel. This has happened once before this century, and we are now at a similar moment in history. And so it is to the choices which this particular time sets before us that we now turn.

9

Evangelicalism, Modernity and Postmodernity

This book has addressed a range of issues facing the church, but the word 'culture' has continued to raise its head. The reason that 'the meeting syndrome' has become such a crippling liability – rather than simply an unbiblical way of 'being church' – is because of the huge culture shift that is happening under our feet in Western (or Westernising) societies. That shift is away from what is usually described as a 'modern' worldview to 'post-modernity'.

The 'modern' period has seen a variety of beliefs and attitudes, of course; terrible wars have been fought between the partisans of some of them. Broadly speaking, however, 'modern' attitudes are characterised by a belief in coherence, logic, unity, principles, abstract ideas, system. Its most important medium of discourse has been the printed text. Sermons and political speeches, which 'piggy-backed' on the mindset that literacy created, could afford to be quite long, complex and substantive.

Postmodernity, on the other hand, is characterised by

preferences for incoherence, experience, diversity, situational ethics, practical techniques and a suspicion of all ideologies. Like the pre-modern ages, postmodernity is more visually oriented, and less literate. Its dominant medium of public discourse is TV. Sermons – and even lessons in school – cannot hope to compete with television in entertainment value (though preachers and teachers have felt constrained to try), and politicians resort to soundbites.[1] Postmodern people have a huge suspicion of all 'metanarratives', by which they mean all overarching explanations of everything. Douglas Adams expressed this suspicion very well: his imaginary computer Deep Thought, after seven and a half million years of calculations, finally came up with the answer to the 'Question of Life, the Universe and Everything': it is '42'. The answer is meaningless because, as Deep Thought went on to point out, the question is meaningless too.[2] Postmodern attitudes tend to regard all metanarratives as vehicles of oppression, the imposition of one group's values and understanding of reality upon all others.

The death of the Marxist dream with the collapse of communism appeared to vindicate this view. Marxism was a classically modernist intellectual construction. It purported to explain all human experience of reality on the basis of some abstract 'scientific' ideas, and to insist that all people would inevitably conform to its teachings

[1] These changes have been brilliantly discussed in N. Postman, *Amusing Ourselves to Death* (Methuen, 1987), pp 41–9, 99–100.

[2] D.Adams, *The Hitch-hiker's Guide to the Galaxy* (Pan, 1979), pp 134–5.

and values. Such an approach to the world strikes post-modern people as frankly incredible. But here's the rub: Christianity is rejected on the same grounds. Whereas many moderns rejected Christianity as untrue (because they believed in Marxism, or the accounts of modern science as conflicting with the Bible, or whatever), post-moderns reject it as being a claim to universal truth.

Christianity purports to give an account of the origins and meaning of the universe, and points to history's ulti-mate fulfilment in the return of Christ. Postmodern thinking rejects such claims as hopelessly totalistic. It is not that Christianity is untrue, but that there is no such thing as truth . . . at least, not of the overarching explan-atory kind that Christianity posits. This way of thinking is a key element in the evangelistic problem of our day. The rejection of moral absolutes makes it hard for people to see themselves as sinners, and certainly makes it difficult for Christians to uphold traditional morality. There also seems to be no way of adjudicating between Christians' religious beliefs and those of the people they are trying to convert: cannot Christianity be 'true' for the Christians and astrology, Hinduism or white witchcraft for somebody else? And as for a final judgement with all people having to give an account for themselves before the Christian God. . . !

Evangelicalism and the culture of modernity

A host of recent Christian writers have sought to respond to objections such as these and, this being a book about how we can 'be church' in our cultural environment, it is

no part of our task (as well as being beyond our compe-
tence) to compete with such authors.[3] But it is certainly
worth reflecting on the extent to which evangelicalism
has been bound up with the culture of modernity. Born
in the eighteenth century, partly as a reaction to the
rationalism of the Enlightenment and partly as a religious form of that very same rationalism, modern
evangelicalism has thrived in societies that are in the
process of becoming literate, and so prize literacy especially highly as an up-and-coming value.[4] Evangelicalism
has clearly been a religion of the book, rather than of the
visual spectacle of a ceremony, such as the mass. Its doctrines tend towards abstract, mental conceptions rather
than visual ones. Justification is by faith (an inner act or
state), rather than by tangible sacraments and visible
good works of the kind that even an illiterate peasant can
appreciate.

Evangelicalism has thrived in societies that are in the
process of urbanising and becoming more commercial.
This was true even in the early modern period before
evangelicalism assumed its modern shape. The English
Lollards of the fifteenth and sixteenth centuries were
mostly artisans and merchants involved in the wool

[3] A.C. Thiselton, *Interpreting God and the Postmodern Self* (T. & T.
Clark, 1995), offers a thoughtful, intellectually formidable response.
G.E. Veith, *Guide to Contemporary Culture* (Crossway, 1994), is more
popular and combative, in the mould of Francis Schaeffer.
[4] On this point, at least, we are more inclined to agree with Dave
Tomlinson's analysis (*The Post-Evangelical*, pp 72–4) than with that of
Graham Cray in G. Cray *et al.*, *The Post-evangelical Debate* (SPCK,
1997), pp 3–4.

trade. The Protestantism of the Reformation, when it came along in the sixteenth century, took hold in the more commercial south and east of England before the north and west, in the towns before the countryside, and among the commercial classes before the peasants or nobility. Even once the country had been forcibly 'converted' from 'popery', the same areas and segments of society that had been protestantised first were the strongest bastions of support for the more virulently evangelical strain represented by Puritanism within the Church of England. This was a division plainly seen when it came to picking sides in the English Civil War of the 1640s. The same, or similar, patterns of distribution hold good for the spread of the various English dissenting groups of the seventeenth century and later.

If one looks at the French Calvinists (or Huguenots), the social demography is even more marked: the movement was dominated by the literate, urban middle classes, especially by lawyers, and made no impression on the peasantry whatsoever.

The real rise of evangelicalism in Britain and America coincided with the Industrial Revolution and the growth on both sides of the Atlantic of an overwhelmingly commercial economy, in which self-reliant families broke free of their kinship ties and moved to towns. The Methodists' greatest gains were in the new factory towns and industrial villages.

Of course, not all countries that have industrialised have become bastions of evangelicalism, but it would be true to say that virtually all strongholds of evangelical Christianity (the USA in the late twentieth century perhaps excepted) have been countries in the process of urbanisation and/or industrialisation. The current rapid growth in much of the urbanising and industrialising Third World is part of the same phenomenon.

Evangelical faith has thrived in societies where nuclear families are prized over wider kinship or tribal groups. In cultures where people can carry logical discourses – such as a well-constructed hour-long sermon – in their heads, there evangelical faith has prospered. These undeniable facts do not mean that orthodox Christianity cannot fare well in any other climate but modernity. Rather, it means that we have to learn to adapt our way of presenting the faith and of 'being church' in non-modern societies. Some things, such as doctrine and biblical knowledge, which were relatively easy to impart in a modernist culture, where literacy was prized and people had little trouble thinking in abstract terms, will need to be treated creatively and worked at harder if they are to be intelligible and appealing to postmodern people. Conversely, visual and experiential elements have far greater potential for conveying the faith – and for leading astray – than was the case in the modern period. Again, presenting the gospel as an all-embracing explanation of 'Life, the Universe and Everything' will pay few evangelistic dividends, even if that's what we think it is. We will do better to focus on practical felt needs and moral applications, and allow people who are in the process of becoming Christians to 'work further in' from there.

In all cases, the onus is where it always has been: upon the evangelists to adapt their presentation to the receptivity of those we seek to persuade. To begin with, 'the authority of Scripture' or 'man's need of a Saviour' is no more intelligible to postmodern people than attacking indulgences and transubstantiation would have been effective in bringing about conversions in the 1960s. We may get people to those points, but they cannot be our opening shots.

'The authority of Scripture' or 'man's need of a Saviour' are, if carelessly explained, easily rejected as 'totalising discourses', and so either dismissed or simply misunderstood and ignored by most people around us. This will be true, not merely of the minority of *cognoscenti* who actually use such trendy phrases as 'totalising discourses' and 'metanarratives', but by non-highbrow and even unreflective people who will simply hear our language as so much impenetrable jargon emanating from an alien conceptual universe. Of course, orthodox Christianity *is* a 'metanarrative'; there is no escaping that, nor should there be any attempt to do so. But the up-front approach to evangelism, and much of our presentation in teaching, has to take account of the actual thought processes of our contemporaries.

We cannot allow our culture-bound presentation of the gospel to become an obstacle to evangelism or discipleship. As Maggi Dawn says,

> To insist on continuity of language and form [means that] Christianity not only becomes alien to those who are not part of it, but it actually changes its meaning for those who are part of it ... We are unavoidably connected to the culture

and language of the world in which we live, and we do not
have the luxury of redefining the terms unless we become a
completely isolated community.[5]

Although she cites the example of the Amish as an extreme
case of cultural fossilisation to the point where the group's
message has become incommunicable to the outside
world, and has completely changed its meaning over the
centuries for its own adherents, she might have pointed
more tellingly to examples closer to home. Almost total
disengagement from culture was widespread, until very
recently, among wide swathes of British and American
evangelicalism, particularly on its fundamentalist wing. If
we are to avoid making ourselves irrelevant by repeating
this error, we have to find ways of expressing the gospel in
the new climate. As usual, resistance to doing what is
necessary is likely to prove strong. As with many organisations and political and religious camps, the tension
between what is acceptable to the internal constituency
and what is needful to gain a hearing with those outside
can be sharp. (One need only think of the Labour Party in
the early 1980s or the Conservatives now.)

Liberal and conservative evangelicals

We have been here before. In the early part of the twentieth century, evangelicalism divided over modernist
issues. The liberal theology of the day (significantly

---

[5] M. Dawn in G. Cray et al., *The Post-evangelical Debate* (SPCK,
1997), p 41.

called 'modernism') was saying, in effect, that orthodox Christianity was not true. Modern science, especially Darwinism, appeared to demonstrate the same. Marxism, then an up-and-coming creed, scornfully rejected all religion on philosophical and political grounds. In facing these issues, evangelicalism divided into two camps: liberal and conservative.

Liberal evangelicals advocated engagement, but actually ended up capitulating to modernist theology. In attempting to salvage what they could of historic Christianity from the depredations of the various modern schools of thought, they ended up with a minimalist 'God of the gaps', a mysterious 'ground of our being', with Jesus as simply a moral teacher whose supposed miracles were really parables. Nineteenth-century evangelicalism had been very strong on social action of various kinds, from charitable work to political campaigns. Partly as a compensatory mechanism for the evacuation of doctrine, and partly to meet Marxist critiques, liberal evangelicalism majored on 'the social gospel' and the espousal of leftish political causes. But by the mid-century liberal evangelicalism had ceased to be genuinely evangelical at all; it had become simply liberal. Several of the traditionally evangelical nonconformist denominations were decimated by this development. Without an evangel, evangelism became impossible. No one was converted to their version of Christianity from unbelief; it became parasitic upon orthodoxy, a sort of refuge for lapsed Christians. The churches that followed this route declined very rapidly and are now little more than shells of what they were in the early 1900s.

The opposite reaction to modernism was adopted by the conservative evangelicals. These were mostly fundamentalists, who insisted upon biblical literalism, especially in respect of the interpretation of early Genesis, as the only secure defence against biblical criticism. They also mostly adopted the novel dispensationalist eschatology[6] which insisted upon a literalist reading of biblical prophecy, drawing the conclusion that the church was supposed to be in decline during the end times (thus justifying their own predicament), and that the Second Coming was to be expected at any moment. Anti-intellectualism, which had for long lurked in the background of some types of evangelicalism, was elevated to the status of positive virtue; modern science and biblical criticism were 'the wisdom of this world', and demonstration of the folly of relying on human reason. Not only was Marxism rejected (with good cause) as so much godless wickedness, but the evangelical social activism of the previous century was also now repudiated: saving souls, not bodies, from the wrath to come was the one thing needful.

Furthermore, the fundamentalists insisted upon rejecting all of the other trappings of modern culture as so much worldliness into the bargain. Cinema, theatre, smoking and drinking were 'out'. So too was dancing. So were modern clothes and modern music such as jazz and, when it emerged, rock and roll.

---

[6] This particular teaching about the end times has its origin in the Brethren movement of the 1830s. Its distinctive hallmark has been the 'any minute rapture' doctrine.

The dualism and unworldliness of this stance, reject-ing social action and intellectual engagement in the interests of 'saving souls', made fundamentalists irrele-vant to their wider culture, an escapist religious ghetto. But they were not the only ones; the capitulation to modernity of the liberals made them irrelevant too. Willing to sing the modernist song in a religious key, they had nothing distinctive – certainly nothing distinctively Christian – to say.

The irony is that both were inescapably 'modern'. The liberals were avowedly modernist in their acceptance of 'scientific' criticism and a basically naturalist worldview. But the conservatives were modernist too: they champi-oned the values of the Victorian age, when evangelical-ism had been at its high water-mark, as a golden era (the golden era is always the one a generation or two before your own). They reflected the 'Scottish Commonsense' school of philosophy emanating from the Enlighten-ment.[7] Dispensationalism claimed, among other things, to treat the biblical texts 'scientifically' by reducing their prophecies to an internally consistent 'system'. Certainly conservatives agreed with modernism in exalting objectivity, though with the important distinctive of seeing God as the underwriter and guarantor of that objectivity. Pre-modern people, by contrast, had tended not to distinguish sharply between subjectivity and objectivity, which is one of the reasons, at least, why mental illness was often considered the work of demons,

---

[7] See G.M. Marsden, *Fundamentalism and American Culture* (OUP, 1980), pp 16–8.

and there was no place for religious or political tolera-
tion. Objectivity as 'a view from nowhere' is a distinctly
modern phenomenon.[8]

In the long run, there seems little doubt that the conservative response to modernity was the lesser evil. The
conservatives at least survived. It is too easy, in retro-
spect, to ridicule the ostrich-like instincts of a generation
or two of believers who lived through one of the greatest
crises to have faced evangelicalism. Even so, it is hard not
to wish that they could have responded more creatively
and imaginatively.

The present situation

With 'the Great Evangelical Recovery of Nerve' since the
Second World War, however, the movement has now
grown and broadened far beyond its fundamentalist
heartland (or origins, one is tempted to say). With
growing self-confidence, conservative evangelicalism has
largely abandoned the dispensationalist doctrines and
the determined out-of-dateness of the early and mid
century. The long, slow process of cultural and intellectual re-engagement has led, among other things, to a
burgeoning and maturing of evangelical theology which,
combined with the obvious tendency of liberal theology
to self-destruct, has left the evangelicals in possession of
much (if by no means yet quite all) of the theological
battlefield. A parallel process has been happening in the

---

[8] Significantly, Francis Schaeffer made the defence of modernist
objectivity an important strand in his apologetic for Christianity.

churches. The growth of evangelicalism, combined with the continuing decline of liberal churches due to their inability to propagate themselves or convert anyone, has left the former in a dominant position. The majority of ordinands within the Church of England (to take a pertinent example) have been evangelical for over a decade now, and the trend shows no signs of abating.

But all is not well. With the spectacular growth has come growing diversity. Though this in itself is welcome, things have reached the point where the very term 'evangelical' has lost its sharpness of definition. In identifying a particular cleric's alignment within a very pluralist denomination such as the Church of England, the epithet 'evangelical' almost always has to be preceded by some qualifier: 'open', 'charismatic', 'reformed', 'traditional', 'moderate' (and, once again, 'liberal'). Although evangelicals of all kinds have traditionally looked to umbrella organisations such as the Evangelical Alliance to represent their joint interests and views, senior leaders among British evangelicals are now wondering aloud how long the camp can be kept together.

Until recently, most evangelicals (in Britain, at least, though not in America) have formed part of a common subculture. The only exceptions were a few groups such as the more exclusive types of Brethren or some Strict Baptists, who mostly chose not to attend conferences, read magazines or co-operate in joint ventures outside of their own group. But now the differences between larger elements of evangelicalism are becoming too great to keep them all together. And this growing apart is coming at the very time when the wider culture of the West is moving into the culture shift that we call postmodernity. That culture shift is raising a whole new range of questions for Christians, and the variety of answers we give to those questions threaten to fragment us further. Since meetings cannot help but reflect the culture and values of those who run them, the centrality of meetings to our way of 'being church' can only serve to widen those fissures, and hasten the process of fragmentation.

10

Alternative Visions

It may be easier to see the urgency of responding to the present cultural shift, and also easier to see the extent to which evangelicalism continues to align itself with a modernist worldview, if we consider the situation in Eastern Europe. The collapse of communism has led to hugely increased opportunities for evangelism but, as discerning evangelicals will have gleaned from the relative silence of the Christian media on the subject, to only moderate growth in numbers. Even that moderate growth is tailing off in many places. Why is this?

Baptists and Pentecostals – the main evangelical battalions in Eastern Europe – have traditionally identified themselves with the West. This is easily understandable. Not only were they founded largely by German and American missionaries, but they looked for pluralist societies in which voluntarist churches of converted believers would not be persecuted. They could not help but be out of sympathy with atheistic communist regimes. However, they also found their identity in conscious contrast to, and rejection of, the Orthodox (and in some countries Catholic) churches, which in the 1930s and 1990s were revealed as representing the tribal gods that justify nationalism. In every case, evangelicals have instinctively supported those political forces in their countries that were opposed to the ex-communists or to nationalism. To that extent, the Western orientation of East European evangelicals is natural, and flows from their ecclesiology. With the flood of Western influences entering Eastern Europe, therefore, one might have expected receptivity to their message to rise much more sharply than it has done.

A closer inspection reveals a more complicated picture. The Western culture that infuses East European evangelicalism is the 'Westernity' of two generations ago. The religious concerns are anti-Catholicism (or anti-Orthodoxy) and biblical inerrancy. Ethics are about teetotalism and not wearing make-up. To attend the services of an average evangelical church is to take a journey backwards in time to a religious culture that existed in Britain in, say, the 1940s or 1950s – certainly before the rise of the charismatic movement and the impact of rock music upon worship. Meetings tend to be led from the front, and churches to be dominated by their pastors, even more than is the case in the West. One young Baptist theologian ruefully described leadership styles: 'Stalinism is alive and well in the Baptist church of my country.' For very understandable reasons in the light of their recent persecutions, evangelicals continue to hold on to the 'bunker mentality' that characterised early and mid-twentieth-century evangelicals in the West.

Of course, this critique on its own could be no more than the myopic naïvety of Westerners astonished at the failure of non-Westerners to be exactly like themselves. That is not our intention. Our point is that, while the religious culture of the churches is perhaps two generations behind the West, the secular culture and its values – particularly those of young people – are perhaps only a decade behind. The values and attitudes that are washing over them like a tidal wave through radio, movies, the press, music and TV are the attitudes of the West today. The result is that the overall ambience of the evangelical churches, which have not even been through the culture shift of the 1960s/70s for the most part, is almost as foreign to young people in, say, Russia or Romania, as it would be to their teenage peers in the West.

One individual case may serve to illustrate the point. Tatiana is a young Russian girl who came to the UK recently to take a one-year course in theology. She was a recent convert, but zealous and, for her age, mature. She was also a gifted artist and highly intelligent. To the disappointment of many who knew her, Tatiana has since decided to return to the Orthodox Church. And the reason? She is one of the most Westernised of Russians; she is not returning with any pre-modern notions of 'Holy Mother Russia' of the kind that may yet appeal to aging peasants. Rather, as a postmodern woman she is appalled at the prospect of the various evangelical churches in her city: ghettos from the world, dualistic in their disengagement from society, smug in their own rightness and everyone else's wrongness, anathematising one another over spiritual gifts or the permissibility of make-up.

By contrast, the Orthodox Church seems 'holistic'. It is engaged with politics and culture. Its worship is visual and aesthetic, not sermonic and print-based. It values art. Eastern Christology and Greek Trinitarian theology are enjoying a vogue in Western theological circles in a way that Russian evangelicals can hardly conceive of – or would even understand, for the most part. The Orthodox churches can thus appeal to the pre-modern – the *babushkas* in the countryside – and the postmodern – like Tatiana, and a generation of Westernised young people like her.

While her decision is eminently understandable, to the eyes of the present writers, it still seems regrettable. Of course the Orthodox Church is 'holistic'. The very nature of its ecclesiology is to embrace the whole of the population – by force, historically, and in its present inclination to restrict religious freedoms in Russia for non-Orthodox. A body whose entire historic mission has been to provide unity between church and people is bound to take politics and art more seriously than evangelicals who have never aimed at being anything other (sociologically speaking) than a sect. But state churches are, to evangelical eyes, simply tribal gods. Christians are called, like Abraham, to forsake their own tribe and their own family in the name of the God of all tribes and all families.[1]

---

[1] M. Volf, *Exclusion and Embrace: a Theological Exploration of Identity, Otherness and Reconciliation* (Abingdon Press, 1996), p 39.

'Going high'

All criticisms of Tatiana's decision aside, however, her move does represent one important possibility which many evangelicals will explore – and are already exploring – during the years that lie ahead. This option might fairly be described as 'going high'. Eastern Orthodoxy, Catholicism and Anglo-Catholicism have much to offer the postmodern mind that is repelled by the abstract wordiness of modernist evangelicalism and attracted by the visual beauty of ceremony and the apparent (though not real) timelessness of liturgy. Perhaps perversely, it is the very archaism of 'high' worship that increases its appeal. The ceremonial, the priestcraft, the hierarchy – which all speak of supposed continuity with another age – are, strictly speaking, equally irrelevant to the *present* experience of everyone. Its irrelevance is, in that sense, a shared quality among old and young, rich and poor alike and so, in a strange way, unifying.

The 'high' option also appears to offer roots to a rootless generation. This point was grasped as long ago as the 1830s with the rise of the Oxford Movement, a high-church rebellion within evangelicalism against the rationalism of the Enlightenment and the ugliness of the Industrial Revolution. These evils were associated by many with what they saw as the squalid matter-of-factness of evangelical nonconformity in its featureless chapels, each one 'a pious warehouse of red brick, with sometimes (but this only in highly ornamented examples) a bell in a birdcage on the top of it'.[2] The new

---

[2] C. Dickens, *Hard Times*, ch 5.

Anglo-Catholicism was thus a harking back to an ideal-
ised (and supposedly static) Middle Ages, a kind of religious counterpart to the novels of Sir Walter Scott, the
paintings of the Pre-Raphaelites and (later) the mock-
Gothic architecture of the late Victorian age – *media eva
rediviva*. Some Christians, like J.H. Newman himself,
the founder of the movement, found their way all the distance back to Roman Catholicism.

The trickle has continued at a steady rate down to the
present. For some who had imbibed too deeply from
liberal biblical criticism, the 'high' ecclesiological doctrines of apostolic succession, priesthood and transubstantiation gave them a new 'place to stand' once their
confidence in Scripture had been shaken. The contacts
which such forms of churchmanship have always kept
open with the cultured and educated élite of society
make them an attractive and respectable option, unlike
the 'sweaty' alternative of brash fundamentalism.
Andrew Walker, leading sociologist and academic of
King's College, London, has turned from his Pentecostal
family roots to Russian Orthodoxy. Franky Schaeffer, son
of the famous apologist Francis, has done the same.
There is a veritable cottage industry of Orthodox
publications in America attempting to proselytise among
disaffected evangelicals. The 'high' churches can appeal
to the pre-modern and the postmodern *against* the
modern. They may have withered somewhat during the
modern period, only to be vindicated by postmodernity.

That is not the whole story, however. Respectfully,
while being understanding of the motives of those
evangelicals who have made this move, or are making it

to some degree, we believe it to be a mistake. In the first place, 'going high' necessarily entails certain key features which fly in the face of the values of most postmoderns. The place of women is an obvious example. Even most modernist evangelicals have shifted their ground on this issue in recent years. The 'high' option entails a practice of church which most would consider retrograde. Indeed, one former leader of the Anglican charismatic movement has turned Eastern Orthodox precisely because he disagrees so strongly with the ordination of women!

Nor is this all. The entire priestly paraphernalia entails a view of church that flies in the face, not simply of fundamentalist tradition, but of the early church and the very meaning of evangelical doctrines of salvation, not to mention modernist and postmodern instincts alike. Furthermore, the historical nature – and to that extent, the very meaning – of such forms of church is to embrace the whole of society, rather than to act as a community of the faithful. While that increases the 'holistic' outlook of such churches, and thus their appeal to postmoderns, the oppressive side of this story becomes evident in those churches' native climes, where – in Eastern Europe at least – they are still the channel for nationalism and the disadvantaging of minorities.[3]

---

[3] Recent attempts at legislation restricting religious freedom of minorities in Orthodox Russia and Bulgaria and in Catholic Croatia come to mind. Similar moves have been made, more or less specifically directed against evangelicals, in both Belarus and Macedonia; the intention is to leave full freedom, and something like a monopoly, to both Orthodox and Catholics.

For these reasons, we believe that 'going high' will have limited appeal, and in the case of many individuals and churches is likely to be a temporary sojourn only, until novelty has worn off and the negative aspects become clear.

Going liberal

A second tendency which, like 'going high', both has a long tradition behind it and some inducement to increase in the present climate, is a tendency to move in a liberalising direction. In some ways, this is the most natural thing in the world. Evangelical institutions have a history of becoming more liberal with the passing of time. Since the evangelical world has never been a monolith but a series of (mostly overlapping) circles of mutual acceptability, the tendency of organisations to 'loosen up' theologically has meant that, with the passage of the years, they have alienated themselves from some of their constituency while taking others with them. In such circumstances, the alienated groups have then often forged out on their own.

The history of OICCU is an excellent case in point. The Oxford Inter-Collegiate Christian Union had its origins in the late nineteenth century and eventually came under the auspices of the Student Christian Movement (SCM). With the growing liberalism of that movement in the opening decades of the twentieth century, evangelicals began to defect, and OICCU was eventually reconstituted by them in 1919, and later linked up with the newly emerged Inter-Varsity Fellowship (IVF, more recently UCCF).

Fuller Seminary is a different kind of example. Originally established in the 1940s as a fundamentalist institution, it has broadened itself immensely. Although it remains one of the premier evangelical institutions in the USA, it would be considered unacceptably liberal by some in the evangelical camp, and would certainly be shunned by adherents of its original fundamentalist constituency.[4] The list of colleges that have followed the same trajectory, to either a greater or lesser degree than Fuller, is a long one.

Individual evangelicals, especially leaders, have often become more liberal during the course of their careers. In the cases of David Jenkins, erstwhile Bishop of Durham, John Habgood, former Archbishop of York, and the academic John Hick – all people who experienced evangelical conversions in their youth – this liberalising process clearly went a very long way and has alienated them, not simply from the more hardline elements within evangelicalism, but from the constituency itself. Of course, from a certain point of view, their careers are simply illustrative of the parasitic nature of liberalism; unable to win adherents from 'the world' it is reduced to feeding off the very orthodoxy it attacks. Were it ever to succeed in destroying orthodoxy, it would then quickly die for lack of a recruiting base!

Our point here, however, is that, just as modernist liberalism arose in response to modernist critiques of

---

[4] The history of Fuller's development is told expertly in G.M. Marsden, *Reforming Fundamentalism* (Eerdmans, 1987).

Christianity, so postmodern critiques are provoking a new liberalising trend. Most evangelicals have shifted their ground over the past two decades on the issue of women's roles in leadership, but the feminist critique is leading to revisionist ideas of gender, of human person-hood, and even of the nature of God. Some hardliners are fighting a rearguard action against any changes at all, but they are a dwindling minority.[5]

The challenge of postmodern thinking is nowhere more evident than in the area of ethics. Michael Vasey's is one of the first voices from within the evangelical camp to indicate that homosexual acts might be morally acceptable.[6] He certainly will not be allowed to feel lonely for long. Others are starting to shift their ground on the necessity of formal marriages. These debates are very complex, and it is not our purpose to enter into them here. The important thing to note is that the ground is, in fact, moving.

Just as the rise of some secular aspects of modernism (biblical criticism, Darwinism, socialism) provoked a split within evangelical ranks, so the rise of postmodern worldviews looks set to do the same, as individuals and churches struggle over what is legitimate cultural accommodation and what is apostasy in respect of crucial gospel content. And, as ever, the issues are muddied, not only by personal differences, but by the unavoidable predicament of being situated in the very mindset we attempt to critique. 'We have the mind of

---

[5] See eg, David Pawson's book, *Leadership is Male* (Highland, 1988).
[6] M. Vasey, *Strangers and Friends* (Hodder, 1995).

Christ' is certainly an aspiration, but seeing our own culture is so difficult precisely because we see *with* it. The modernists – whether liberal, evangelical or secular – were wrong; there is no 'view from nowhere', only a variety of possible views from here. Even revelation comes mediated.

The effect upon meetings of a liberalising theology will certainly be to dampen down enthusiastic worship (say, of a charismatic type), since the religious certainty implicit in such a style would inevitably be stigmatised as 'triumphalist'. Where would that leave Christian meetings? Back to hymn sandwiches? Maybe. But perhaps the case of Dave Tomlinson himself is instructive. All his protestations to the contrary, his 'post-evangelicalism' has certainly entailed a 'new liberalism' in response to postmodern issues, as his statements concerning homosexuality and marriage make plain.[7] For him, the journey began by moving from his house-church roots to an ultra-informal, even anarchic, form of church – Holy Joe's, which was essentially a discussion group meeting in a pub. But it has ended (at least for the moment!) with a move in exactly the opposite direction: he has become a clergyman in that most institutionalised of churches, the Church of England.

No slight here is intended to Anglican evangelicals; we are discussing only directions of movement. We suspect that, as for many liberals, a shift to a 'higher' ecclesiology or acceptance of greater institutionality than they personally held to before is a compensatory mechanism

---

[7] D. Tomlinson, *The Post-Evangelical* (SPCK, 1995), pp 35–6, 39.

for the evacuation of traditional theological content. (In the same way, 'liberal' Baptists tend to be more denominationally minded and prefer meetings of more principled formality than their theologically more conservative peers precisely *because* of their own less strident theology.)

So the liberal option, like 'going high', leads towards more structured meetings, and towards greater institutionality. Like the old, modernist liberalism, it seeks 'relevance' to the thought-world of the outside culture to the point of capitulation to it, and then leans on an outmoded and irrelevant culture of 'being church' to give itself at least some kind of coherent identity. At the risk of being judgemental, we suggest that this is a bad idea!

'Going mystic'

For many Christians, the perceived insensitivity and stridency of traditional evangelicalism can be minimised – or even eliminated – without obvious compromise or defection to the 'high' or 'liberal' camps. Recent years have seen a noticeable resurgence of contemplative spirituality. The popularity in the 1980s of the Quaker Richard Foster's classic, *Celebration of Discipline*, was both creative and indicative of a trend.[8] Contemplative and devotional writers from other traditions, like Henri Nouwen and Ronald Rolheiser, are now bestsellers in the evangelical market. And this is doubtless as it should be. The long-time evangelical obsession with preachiness

---

[8] R.J. Foster, *Celebration of Discipline* (Hodder, 1980).

and activism often came at the expense of cultivating a relationship with God or of personal spiritual transformation. The result was frequently a triteness and blandness about evangelical statements which did little to recommend the gospel.

Nevertheless, the shift comes as part of an overall trend in Western mindsets in favour of examining the inner life, and a turning to psychology and esoteric spiritual techniques. To that extent, it is not without its dangers. The growing interest in contemplative spirituality, while acting as a healthy corrective, certainly has the capability, if taken very far, to stifle the very activism and 'conversionism' that have been the evangelical movement's vital strengths, and have allowed it to continue to reproduce itself even in hostile social environments.

Likewise, the mysticism of New Age thinking has a tendency to subvert even those who believe themselves to be consciously rejecting it. (Origen, a theologian of the early church, found the same problem with Platonism.) That is because, as we have said, it is so hard to discern the influences we unconsciously absorb from our own culture because we see *with* that culture and its prejudices. It is difficult not to conclude that the complex cosmologies required by some recent evangelical trends (such as 'deliverance ministries' and the interest in 'territorial spirits' together with their attendant brands of 'spiritual warfare') do owe something, at least, to New Age fascination with the esoteric. These trends are dualist and, to a cynical eye, may reflect evangelical frustration at the difficulty of evangelising their neighbours; the response is a turning within and, in the process, tackling the allegedly underlying spiritual causes. The recent toying with 'creation spirituality' and green issues, by contrast, represents a more self-conscious acceptance of trends within the wider society. When exploring this area, most evangelicals at least have their eyes open, and can choose for themselves how far they wish to go.

The implications of this trend for evangelical meetings culture is unclear, since the consequences are as various as the causes. An emphasis upon contemplative spirituality is likely to lead to a very different kind of worship, probably 'high', and a de-emphasis upon the sermon, certainly in its traditional, authoritarian form. Deliverance ministries and the new forms of 'spiritual warfare', however, are likely to reinforce triumphalism and sensationalist meetings, along with declamatory styles of preaching.

Combining the options

It will already be apparent that the options we have mentioned – 'going high', 'going liberal' and 'going mystic' – are by no means mutually exclusive. The growing craze for 'Celtic spirituality' is a prime example of mingling the first and third of these possibilities. The Celtic church has the supreme virtue of no longer being around; whatever values are projected back onto it cannot be contradicted by current or recent experience. Even better, the sources about it are relatively scarce compared with those for, say, the medieval Catholic church, so the opportunities for cutting out the past in our own shape are almost limitless. Much of the material on this subject that has recently been published is certainly very helpful and valuable, especially the devotional writings. But this does not alter the reality that the Celtic churches were simply a variant form of early medieval Catholicism, with a much greater place for monasticism, particularly of the eremitic (hermit) variety, a different form of tonsure and a different date for celebrating Easter. They were also even more heavily into asceticism than their Roman cousin. And there the substantial differences end. To make them a precursor of modern feminism and the Green Movement, as some have done, is little short of laughable. The present authors are naturally disposed to think more than kindly of all things Celtic – one of us has been a member of the Welsh Language Society and a Plaid Cymru voter. But even we are sufficiently modernist to believe that the actual historical data – concerning the Celtic church or anything else – cannot simply be distorted at will.

Our objections notwithstanding, the 'Celtic' fad probably has some little way to run yet – though most likely not, alas, as far as doing something constructive like actually learning Welsh and evangelising Caernarfonshire! The fad is connected with its secular New Age counterpart that leads English hippies to select Ceredigion as the preferred site for their tepee encampments and English environmentalists to choose Machynlleth as the ideal location for their Centre for Alternative Technology. The inspiration for resurgent paganism owes more to romanticism about the Celtic past – Merlin, Stonehenge and the Druids – than to medieval English 'cunning-men' or the lore of the Saxon Hwicce.

Other combinations of our options are possible. The ill-fated Nine O'clock Service (NOS) is an example – albeit one that went horribly wrong – of an attempt to combine highly iconic worship (of a very hi-tech variety) with an increasingly liberal approach to the theological agenda thrown up by postmodernity. Despite its nemesis, others show signs of being determined to follow in its wake, minus the glaring defects. We are disposed to think that there may be considerable value in this, certainly if the theological concessions remain within the bounds of orthodoxy. But the resources and expertise to put on the kind of 'show' that is entailed will be available in only a very few instances. Surely what is necessary in the longer term is to find ways of being creative and relevant in worship that do not depend on large budgets and that encourage participation rather than passivity?

Staying the same: 'modernist fundamentalism' or. . . ?

There is one further option that is likely to appeal to many within the evangelical fold, and this we can dub 'modernist fundamentalism'. By this we mean an absolutising of the modernist cultural norms that are palpably passing away around us. It will probably include the old fundamentalism; that is, a reliance upon a literalist biblical hermeneutic. But it will certainly emphasise the institutional importance of the local church (and thus of meetings), the central place of preaching and the inferior position of women. Its defence of traditional morality will be expressed in terms of abstract 'moral absolutes' as opposed to 'moral relativism', thus relying on the modernist hermeneutic of 'a view from nowhere' (or, as they will insist, 'a view from God'). There will be an inclination to authoritarianism as the only counterbalance to the constant instability of congregations and tendency of members to move on that we see at present.

Most importantly it will represent its own, dated version of modernist evangelicalism as normative, historical Christianity, free from cultural accretions. Such claims will be nonsense, of course, for the only cultural accretions from which it will really be free will be those of the surrounding culture. It will be back to a case of being spiritual and faithful by being two generations out of date. As Jaroslav Pelikan, perhaps the greatest living historian of Christian doctrine, has pointed out,

> The perennial warnings of theologians about philosophical speculation as an activity dangerous to sound doctrine invariably come in the name of a 'sound doctrine' that was the product of speculation and that has incorporated elements of some other philosophical perspective.[9]

We propose that all of the options we have described here are, to say the least, less than optimal. Some are likely to be disastrous. If evangelicalism increasingly fragments, as we believe it will, it is the 'modernist fundamentalists'

---

[9] J. Pelikan, *The Vindication of Tradition* (Yale University Press, 1984), p 67.

who will win out in the long term, as the original fundamentalists did eventually after the last great parting of
the waters in the early twentieth century. That may be an
unpalatable fact, but despite all their shortcomings, they
will at least keep the essence of the gospel sacrosanct,
even if vested in pointlessly alien clothes for a generation
or two. Eventually, despite themselves, they will do
exactly what they say they are refusing to do: they will
accommodate themselves to their surrounding culture,
at least sufficiently for their words to have some evangelistic effect. The liberals and the mystics will have exactly
the same evangelistic effect on their contemporaries that
modernist liberalism had before them: that is, precisely
none whatsoever. They will maintain themselves only in
a parasitic relationship on the orthodox until eventually
even that is undercut by the resurgence of the latter.

When shall these things come to pass? Who knows,
but the third quarter of the twenty-first century might be
a fair bet for the wheel to have come full circle. The fragmentation is already underway. And if truth will triumph
in the end, an awful lot can happen before *that*! If all this
sounds like the gloomiest of prophecies, it may be that
there is not an inexorable fate that comes upon people
however they act, but there certainly is one that comes
upon them *unless* they act. The wasteland in which
evangelicalism has lived for so much of this century need
not be repeated, but it will be if the posturing that is
going on now continues.

What is needed is an adaptation both of the cultural
forms of 'being church' and of the way in which we
express the gospel without compromise of the message

itself. This book is concerned primarily with the first of these, with the way we choose to 'be church'. The heart of our problems in the new culture that is emerging is concerned with meetings and their centrality to our church life. It is that centrality that needs to be challenged. But it is precisely this that is a non-negotiable factor to traditionalists and 'progressives' alike; the institutionality of church is taken for granted.[10] We contend that it is only by deconstructing our institutions – not completely, of course, but to a greater extent than most of us have been willing to allow – that we can become relevant in a postmodern culture that is so distrustful of power relationships. Furthermore, by doing this we can resolve a good many of our own internal conflicts at the same time. We have to change to remain the same.

We can see this last point from experience. Many nineteenth-century Mennonites sought to retain in exact detail the forms of their sixteenth-century Anabaptist heritage. In so doing, they failed to be the Anabaptists of *their* century. That task, if it was done by anyone, was

---

[10] See, for example, the assumption of churchly institutionality as a given in W. Brueggemann, *The Bible and Postmodern Imagination* (SCM, 1993), p 24: 'The purpose of preaching and of worship is transformation. We undertake theater that is potentially life-changing . . . This dramatic moment intends that people should go away changed, perhaps made whole, perhaps savaged.' These words, from a 'progressive', could be echoed by almost all traditionalists. 'How,' he asks, 'do people change?' Not, we suggest, by 'the meeting' in a culture which is supercharged with emotional moments, and the next catharsis only as far away as a powerful TV programme.

achieved by the Brethren and some of the other radical groups of the day. But by the twentieth century, some of these had become so rigid that the role they had fulfilled was assumed instead by the Pentecostals and latterly, perhaps, by the house churches. Some, at least, of these are now in danger of ossifying, with leaders who insist on being true to the 1970s right on into the 1990s and 2000s. We have to change to remain the same. It is time to consider, at last, what the nature of that change might be.

11

Shaping Tomorrow

Not renowned for its ability to anticipate change and be ahead of the game, the church's stance has frequently been one of responding to changes that have already taken place in an attempt to reclaim ground that has already been lost. The challenge for the future is whether or not we can be proactive, rather than simply reactive.

Many churches have lamented the passing-away of the traditional Sunday school. It grew out of an era when Sunday schools were precisely what they describe themselves as being: school on a Sunday, an opportunity for instruction in the two R's – writing and religion. As levels of literacy improved through the provision of universal education, their role changed and many saw them as the place where children could receive a grounding in sound Christian morality, and along the way pick up lots of good Bible stories. There was something quite wholesome about sending children along to Sunday school. They also served as well-stocked and productive fishing grounds for many churches who seized the opportunity to evangelise. The product of such a process, one of the authors began in the youngest group (or 'class' as it was called) at the age of five. Finding himself a Christian by thirteen he was actively involved in the church soon after. The following thirty years are part and parcel of a personal spiritual history, but it was Sunday school that played a major role right there at the beginning.

During the past forty years the institution of Sunday school, certainly as it once was expressed, has all but ceased to exist. Enormous changes have taken place in society at large and for a whole range of reasons the traditional Sunday school no longer has the same appeal. Very few anticipated the trend before it began and, once the decline in attendance started to take effect, it became impossible to reverse. Innovative attempts have been made more recently by groups such as the Salvation Army as they have established Sunday schools in supermarkets, a creative response (in the spirit of their founder) to take the message to people where they are.

This book has commented on 'the meeting syndrome' and the dangers of failing to recognise weaknesses inherent in such a condition. Change has taken place and will continue to do so. We are already witnessing an increasing level of disillusionment with church and a growing number of Christians who are either casualties of some of the difficulties that have been highlighted in the previous pages, or simply unable to find an expression of church with which they are able to identify. For many others, who have never been Christians, church culture is strangely alien and inaccessible, hindering rather than aiding an understanding of the gospel. Outside the church the rate and pace of change is remarkable, making John Stott's call for 'double listening' critically important.

> We listen to the Word with humble reverence, anxious to understand it, and resolved to believe and obey what we come to understand. We listen to the world with critical alertness, anxious to understand it too, and resolved not necessarily to believe and obey it, but to sympathise with it and to seek grace to discover how the gospel relates to it.[1]

Without a commitment to this two-way listening we will experience great difficulties in responding rightly to the needs and challenges facing the church right now.

Rather than waiting and attempting to deal with the results of collapse, the opportunity ahead is one which allows us to respond creatively. Far from reaching the end of the road, we have the opportunity to go further. Much of what we have highlighted has shown there is a real need for change and our plea is that the issues which have been identified are responded to in ways that empower and enable ordinary Christians to be better disciples of Jesus.

Without a doubt the future will be characterised by diversity, and this in itself will be a challenge to some sections of the church more used to uniformity and to what is sometimes mistakenly called 'singleness of vision'. If we are truly to reach the multi-cultural and multi-ethnic people who populate our society then we must be prepared, not only to accept and tolerate churches which

---

[1] John Stott, *The Contemporary Christian* (IVP, 1992), p 28.

look quite unlike our own, but actively to encourage those whose call is to 'be church' where they are.

The popularity of Cell Church is a promising phenomenon, understandably seized on by some far-sighted leaders as a way of mobilising and involving the church body more effectively. The primary aim of each cell is to reproduce and – working on the basis of small groups of people who share a common interest or occupation, who are from a particular age range or who belong to the same cultural grouping – it is being heralded by some as a way of church planting in areas previously devoid of indigenous churches. Unlike housegroups, which have become standard mid-week groupings for a large number of churches (even those who would have seen themselves as ardent opponents of the original movement which spawned the housegroup), Cell Church is built around the life of the cell itself, which becomes the foundational building block of the church. Larger gatherings happen less frequently because they are not quite so important in the week-to-week life of the church. Such, at least, is the theory. Worship, prayer, pastoral care and evangelism all feature as essential components of the cell and leaders are given comprehensive training and support. The focus is clearly not meant to be the large meeting. Some of the teaching materials about Cell Church do, however, advocate a highly structured and formula-driven approach to the weekly cell meetings.

It will be interesting to see what emerges from those who have been pioneering in this field as the model is adjusted and adapted to different cultural settings. We anticipate that the more formulaic and technique-oriented versions of Cell Church will experience both faster early growth (because of their take-up by existing Christians) and earlier stultification than those versions which allow for gradual, organic development.[2] It is these latter, however, which are more likely to bear fruit in the long run, as they allow each group to adapt to local needs and the personal strengths of the individuals involved.

Unquestionably the interest in Cell Church is a good thing. For many it has grown out of an awareness that the church in general (and, for the leaders who have adopted the model, their church in particular) needs to examine the way it operates. The space and opportunity created, the re-ordering of priorities concerning meetings and the level of empowerment possible all make this a move in the right direction. Much will remain dependent on the level of understanding there is within the initiating Christian community, particularly if it has been used to functioning differently. Structural re-organisation can only work effectively when it is born out of a change in understanding and thinking. Housegroups and a

---

[2] In exactly the same way, those house churches which were most successful initially (i.e. in the 1970s and early 1980s) were those whose leaders organised their churches most assiduously and forcefully around their own new insights, principles and techniques. The networks which have prospered in the long term, however, have been those which have taken a less messianic attitude towards their own distinctives, and have been content to encourage pragmatic applications, suitable to local constraints, and to promote 'general directions' of movement, rather than sacrosanct techniques and their own institutional structures.

worship band have failed to revive many a church due to the fact that something far more radical was needed, often regarding the understanding of church itself. The vanquishing of the old by the young was never the answer to any church's problem. Rather, we need multi-faceted approaches which take the venom out of the culture clashes endemic in meeting-centred churches and find creative, bridge-building ways of incarnating church to the countless subcultures that constitute the society we are called upon to reach with the gospel.

The question of cultural relevance has already been touched on and remains a major issue the church must tackle. Far from being simply an evangelistic strategy, what is at stake here strikes at the heart of the gospel: reaching people from every tongue and tribe and nation. Culture and identity are inextricably bound together.

Those who have been involved in planting churches in youth culture have found it important to create opportunities for people to become Christians without having to jettison their own culture completely and become integrated into something that is often very foreign. The originators of Remix, a partnership of four or five groups pioneering in this area, have advocated the importance of breaking the moulds and stereotypes in worship, in styles and approaches to teaching and in the recognition of leadership in the young. What is emerging is still in the formative stages and will doubtless continue to be quite fluid for some time to come. (But then, fluidity is where we are all heading!)

There has been a heated debate about similar issues relating to university campuses in Britain as Fusion, an organisation aiming to establish cells accountable to local churches in universities, has been launched. Once again the question of cultural relevance has been a key issue lying behind the formation of this group.

The struggles to reach the vast majority of a generation who are either deeply suspicious of church as an institution or for whom it has no relevance whatsoever seem set to continue. Simon Jones, former editor of the magazine *Christianity*, makes some helpful comments arising out of his experiences and observations:

> Younger people these days don't go overboard on participatory activities. Most of the hymn-writers and leaders of today's churches grew up in the fifties, sixties and seventies and came to faith in the midst of an explosion of 'body life' in the churches. Everyone wanted to join in, participate, have a rôle in getting things done. They have been succeeded by a generation which, for good or ill, takes a more detached view of participation, hangs back from involvement, wants genuine relationships, but does not want to be asked to sing with strangers.[3]

Amidst some controversy, the church in the 'youth culture' camp say they are responding to the needs of a generation who are unchurched and highly unlikely to respond to traditional methods of evangelism.

Some of the key figures in this movement cite their own experiences as full-time evangelists touring the country in rock bands, taking week-long missions in schools and colleges up and down the country. Their

---

[3] Simon Jones, *Struggling to Belong* (IVP, 1998), p 34.

experience was that, while there was often a good response from teenagers wanting to know more about the Christian faith, by the end of the week only a handful actually made it through to finding faith themselves and becoming a part of a local church. Even those who had become Christians by the end of the week struggled to find a church where they felt at home. Undoubtedly some of the fall-off from a week's mission could be put down to the fact that the band had left and that interest had inevitably waned, but that isn't the whole story. Their own research revealed the startling finding that children found it most difficult to relate to the newer churches which had, in the last generation, prided themselves on being contemporary. More traditional churches had recognised that young people would be unlikely to relate to the way they did things and had provided alternatives. Newer churches, it seemed, were slower to wake up to the truth!

For the youth-culture evangelists, there seemed little alternative other than to create churches that were 'friendly' to young people. Accused of dividing the church, of heresy and sheep-stealing (echoes of the past?), the enthusiasts for youth-culture churches were undeterred. Youth churches, congregations and initiatives have sprung up across the country and are often places of life, creativity and growing faith as younger people take up the challenge to contextualise the gospel in their own culture.

Festivals, regional 'events' and club nights have followed and show little sign of abating. Heavily dependent on the technological hardware and expertise of the culture, these events are beyond the resources of the average youth group, yet a portable CD player, some candles and a little imagination are serving some groups well!

It would be an error, however, to limit the need for cultural relevance to youth culture, for there are many cultures and subcultures within the context of British society that are crying out for an incarnation of church, not as stand-alone congregations, but drawn in to be part and parcel of the wider church. Disapproval, suspicion and mistrust will lead to an unnecessary separation, impoverishing both established churches and those beginning to move out. It is a time, instead, for us to give our blessing and our support to those who are embarking on new ventures.

Of course, the pursuit of relevance can be dangerous as, without care and wisdom, the distinctives of a Christian lifestyle and values can be lost. Mike Pilavachi, pastor of Soul Survivor, Watford, sees this very clearly:

> There are certain things that we are meant to be counter-cultural about. When the early Christians translated Jesus' words from Aramaic they changed the packaging but they left the gift intact. While Jesus changed the stories, he never deviated from the message he came to give. The message is a challenge to many aspects of culture; instead of selfishness it talks about generosity; instead of sexual freedom it talks about purity; instead of death being a kind of nothingness it talks about heaven and hell. Sometimes we are meant to be prophetic to the culture, not to be so absorbed in it we are indistinguishable from it.[4]

---

[4] Mike Pilavachi, *Live the Life* (Hodder, 1998), p 134.

In stressing the strengths of cell churches and youth congregations, the very last thing we wish to suggest is that these strategies alone hold the key to the future. The whole point of postmodernity is that there is no 'only' any more! Whatever the two of us say, meeting-centred, institutionalised churches will undoubtedly continue to exist and to do much valuable work. They may even pro-liferate. Our guess is, however, that they will continue to fragment and that a huge proportion of the nervous, social, moral and physical energies of the participants will be consumed wastefully in struggles over the culture, content and leadership of meetings. Conversely, those churches which find ways of reducing that friction to a minimum and of releasing their members into gainful employment are likely to reap the benefits even if, by their very nature as minimally institutional entities, they retain a fairly low visibility.

In approaching the diverse future where church will need to be expressed in many ways, where people will need to have the opportunity not only to know, love and respond to God in their own culture but also to meet as part of the wider body of the church, there are two dis-tinct priorities to keep in focus.

The call away from self-centredness

Whatever shape the future takes, we must aim to create a church which engenders a genuine sense of communal-ity, encouragement, trust, friendship and confidence. The loss of these things often results in a crisis of confidence and a fear of waste and pointlessness.

Cynicism and disillusionment can so easily rob the
young and the forward-thinking of any real desire to
move the church along. Reluctant to saddle themselves
with the structures, forms and labels of the past, they
often struggle to find a context for their own thinking.
We must do all we can to help provide that context.
History would be very different if some of the individuals and movements who were forced to work outside the
church because of opposition from within had been
backed and supported earlier on in their development.

The issue of relationships is central. We must resist
allowing ourselves to become detached from each other
and then fail to see that as a crisis. To learn to live with
detachment is the greatest tragedy of all. 'Relationships
are the most central factor of our very existence as
human beings.'[5] And the fact that our track record would
seem to indicate that we are little better at handling them
than those who are not Christians, points to our need to
rethink and prioritise. Francis Schaeffer put it like this:

> Unless people see in our churches not only the preaching of
> the truth but the practice of the truth, the practice of love
> and the practice of beauty; unless they see the thing the
> humanists rightly want but cannot achieve on the humanist
> base – human communication and human relationship – is
> able to be practised in our communities, then let me say it
> clearly: they will not listen and they should not listen.[6]

---

[5] Tom Marshall, *Right Relationships* (Sovereign World, 1992), p 9.
[6] Cited in Gene A. Getz, *Sharpening the Focus of the Church* (Victor, 1984), p 273.

We stand in need of expressing unity in our differences, even as we express the one gospel in glorious, creative diversity.

The enormously successful Alpha course offers one way to connect with others in a semi-formal environment. There is a chance to build relationships, to ask questions and to make progress on the journey towards faith. Undoubtedly the fact that food and drink play such a prominent role in the course also helps to establish the right sort of ambience and relational context. The teaching content is well thought out and clearly communicated. The key factor, however (other than the Holy Spirit!), is the opportunity to begin friendships and experience being a part of a community of believers. And if people begin to feel that they belong it is often not long before they come to believe.

Maybe it's time to change our thinking and make our church communities more inclusive and accessible, welcoming those with questions and lifestyles that aren't quite sorted yet. We need to recreate a 'fringe'! Spirituality is certainly on the agenda outside of the church, as the past few years have seen a mushrooming of interest in a wide range of alternatives to standard church fare – golden opportunities for the church to be creative in its appeal to those who are searching for the genuine article.

The importance of being organic

Secondly, church must reflect its parts, not vice versa. It's so very easy for a church to be governed and controlled by a whole weight of expectations placed upon it by tradition, by leaders and by its own history.

One church known to us is certainly not lacking in vision. Having begun relatively recently they have taken on board an ambitious community project initiating a number of 'business in the community' pilot schemes, a second-hand baby clothing outlet and a liaison with the local Probation Service in working with people who are trapped by chemical dependency – plus a whole host of other projects. Not an enormous church, they have only been able to launch each project as the key initiators have come forward. Without these the projects have had to wait. It has certainly focused prayers as the leaders have resisted trying to carry everything themselves and fought back the temptation to pressurise members of the congregation into accepting responsibility for things for which they quite clearly do not have the enthusiasm or the gifting. The recognition of who it is who makes up the church and what they have a calling to be and do is liberating for a body of people as they work out what it means to 'be church' together.

Future models of church need to have values which have been shaped by history and tradition, but not controlled and limited by outdated cultural expressions of those traditions. The strength of any Christian community will, to a large extent, be dependent on the willingness of its members to interact with the historic knowledge and wealth of the people of God. But if what we experience is *merely* an adherence to form, or the unthinking acceptance of an interpretation passed down, then before too long we will discover an inability to meet the challenge of 'being church' in the twenty-first century. It simply isn't good enough for a spiritual heritage and legacy to be passed on and blindly taken on board. There must be understanding born out of an opportunity to question and examine, to think and re-think from within that heritage.

Finally (at the risk of stating the obvious), whatever forms the future church experiments with and whatever expressions emerge during the next five or ten years, it is vital that we recognise Jesus as the head of the church and remain rightly focused. No initiative, project or vision will be an adequate replacement for the dynamic of a living relationship with Jesus himself. And after all, it is he who will build his church!